Vitality Tattoo
The Tattoo Art of Shannon Schober
Volume II

Vitality Tattoo Volume II

The Tattoo Art of Shannon Schober

Copyright (C) 2009

Vitality

*1240 Brevard Rd
Suite 1
Asheville NC
28806*

ISBN 978-0-9818677-2-4

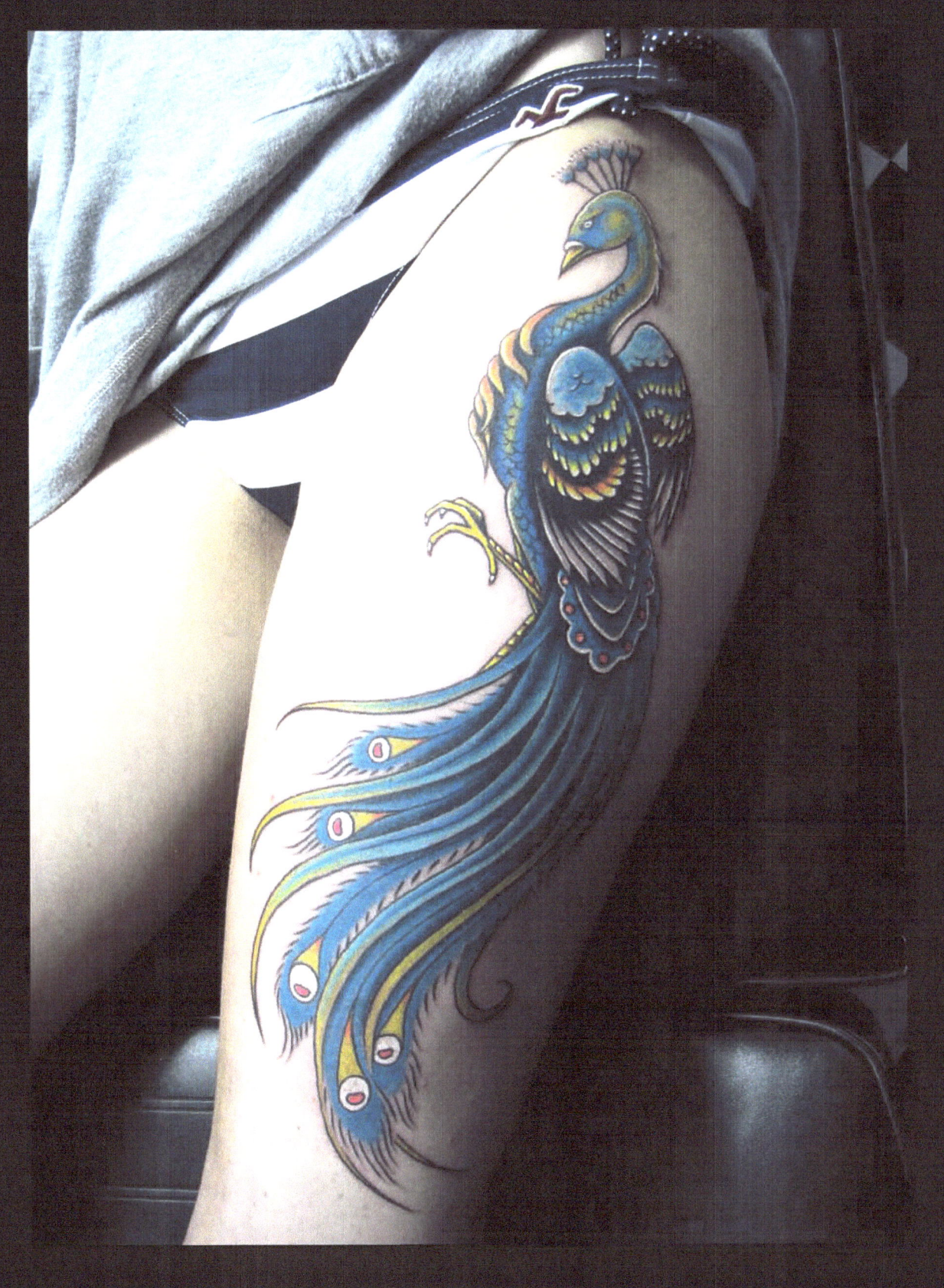

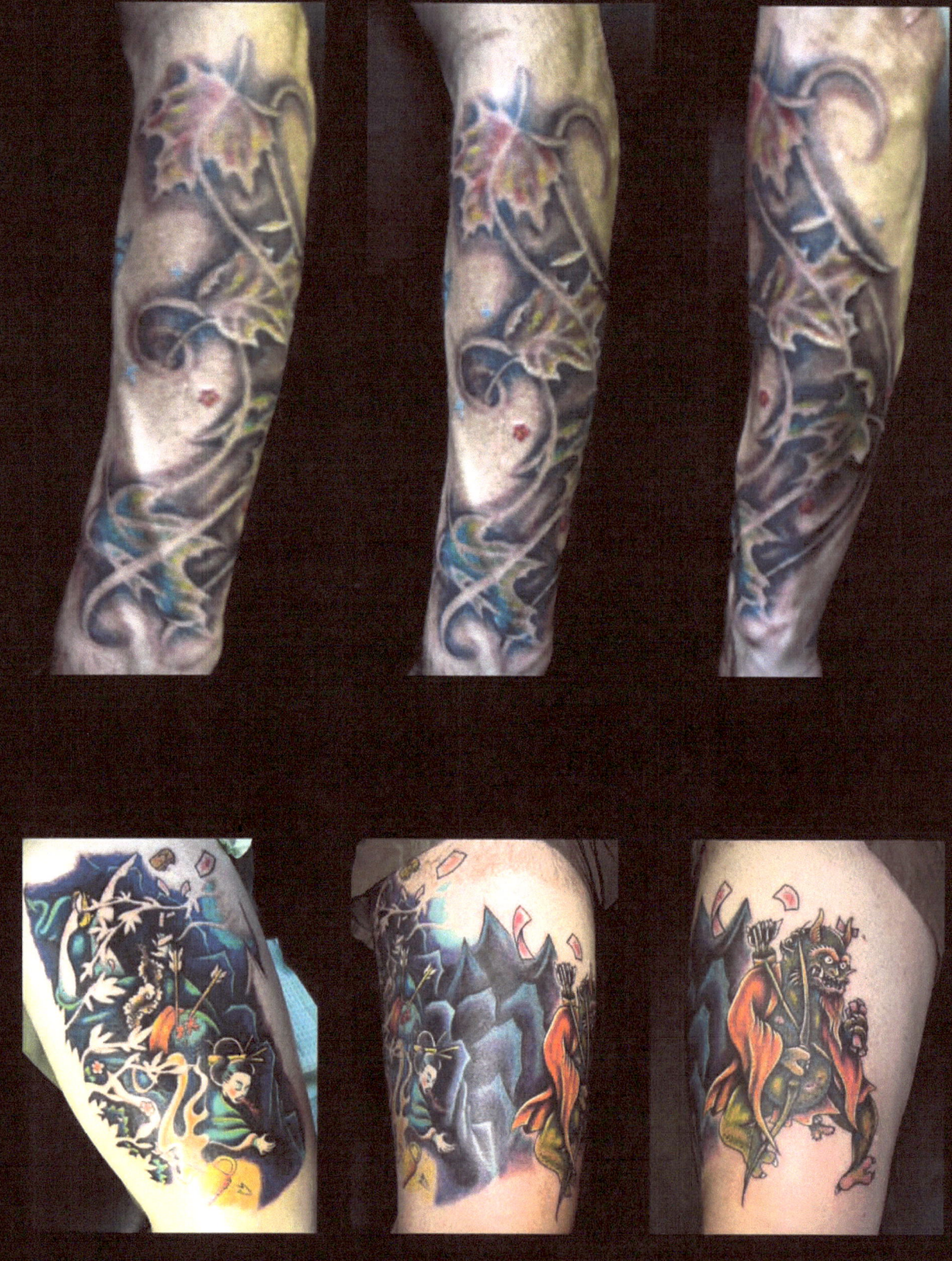

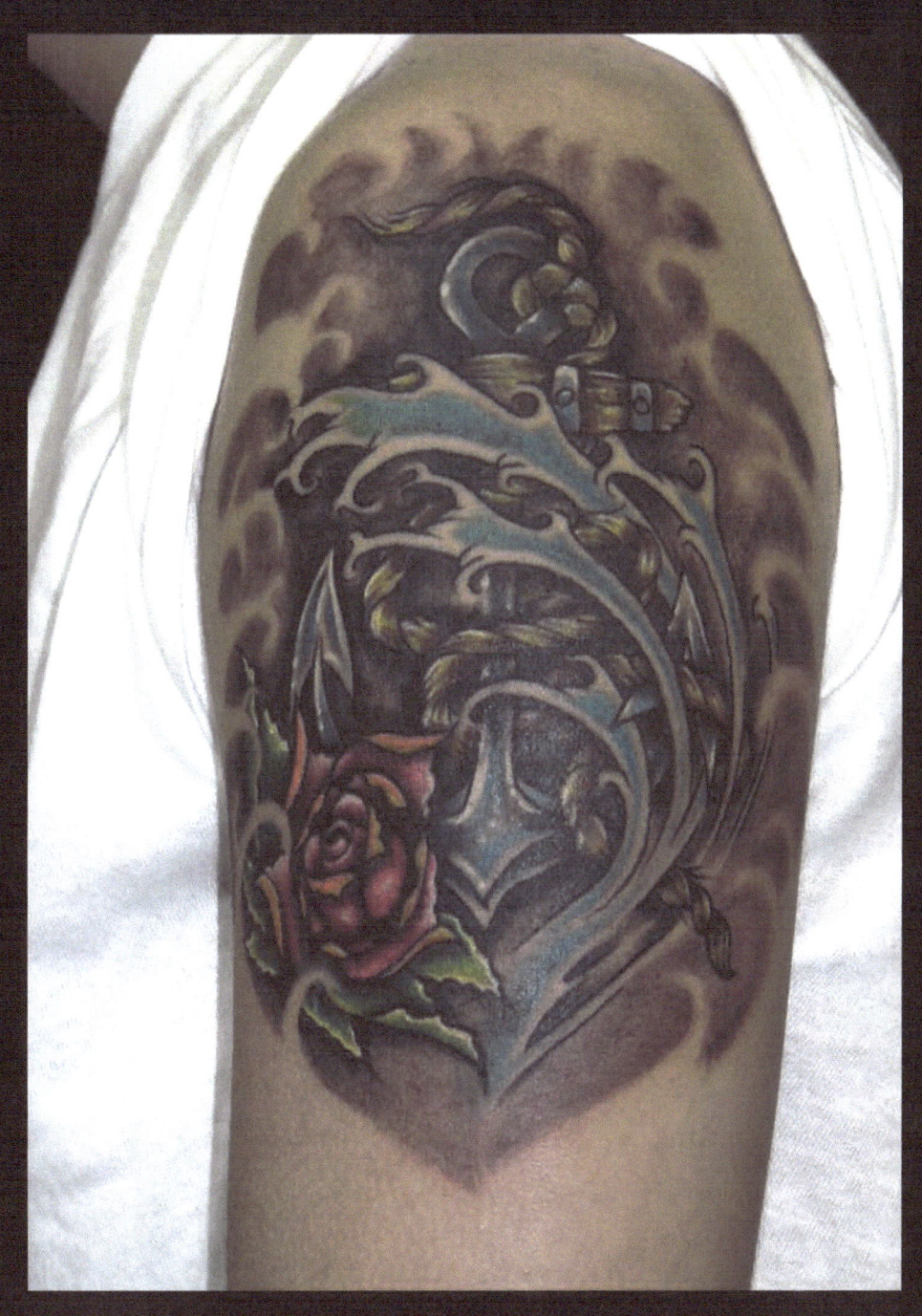

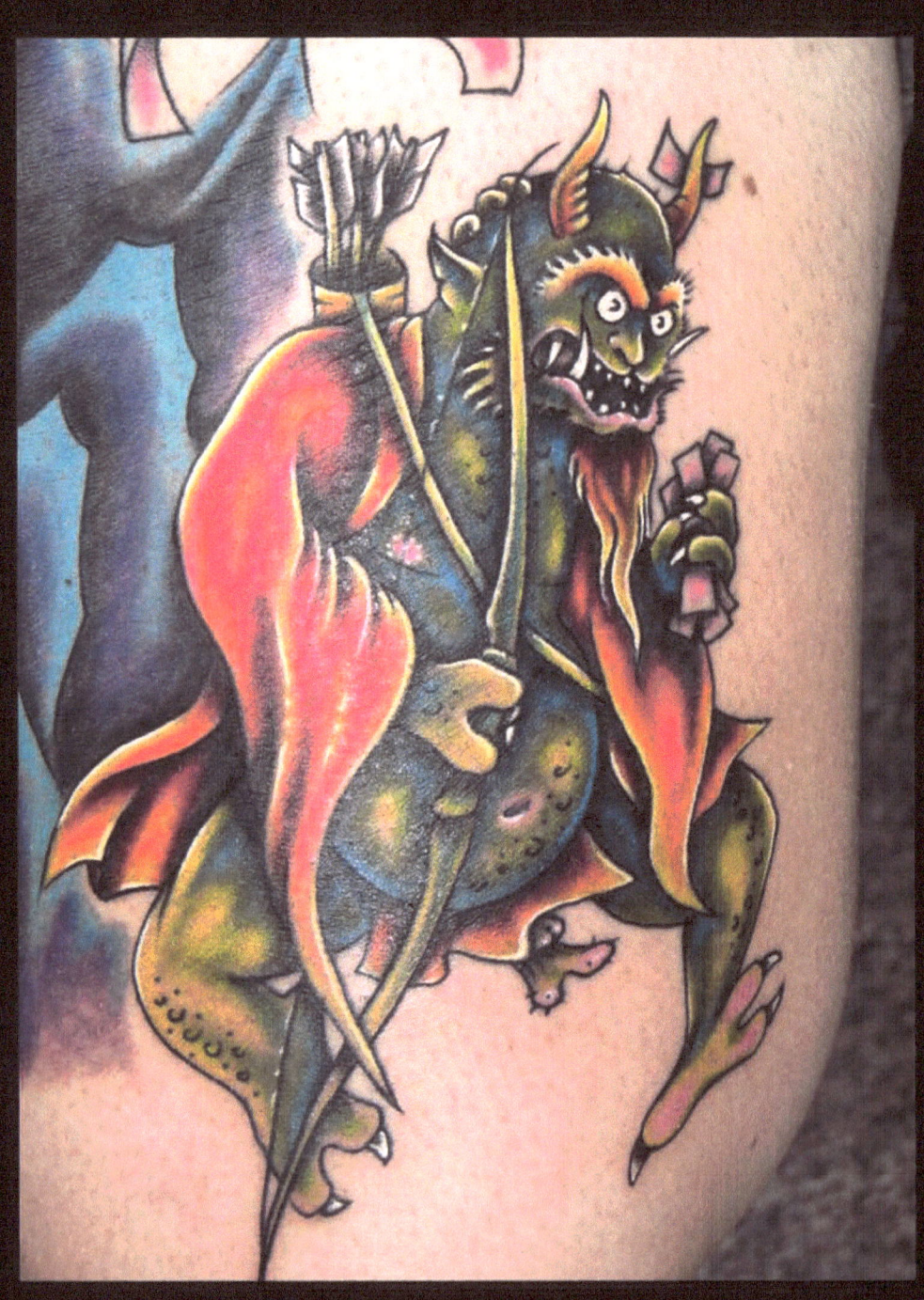

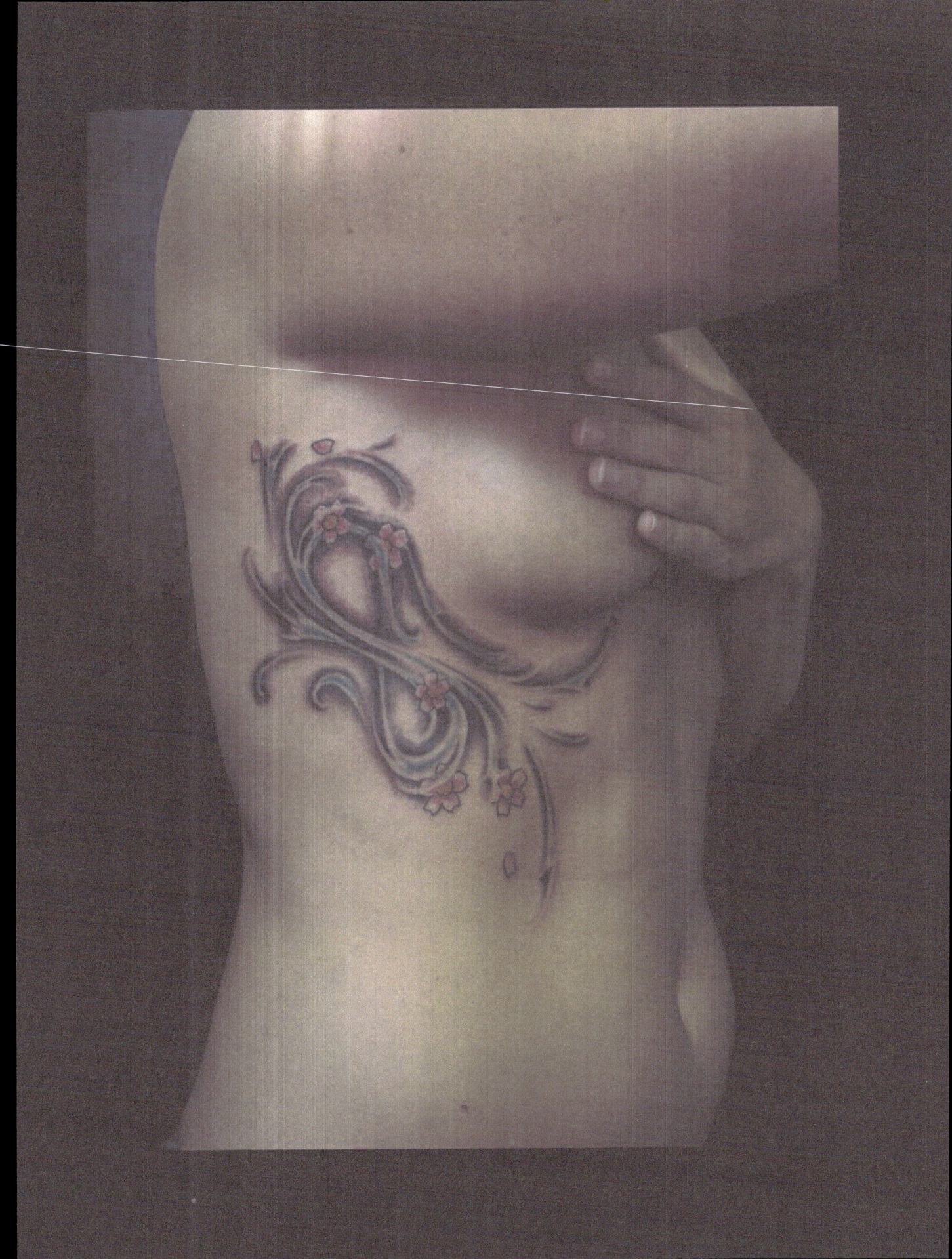

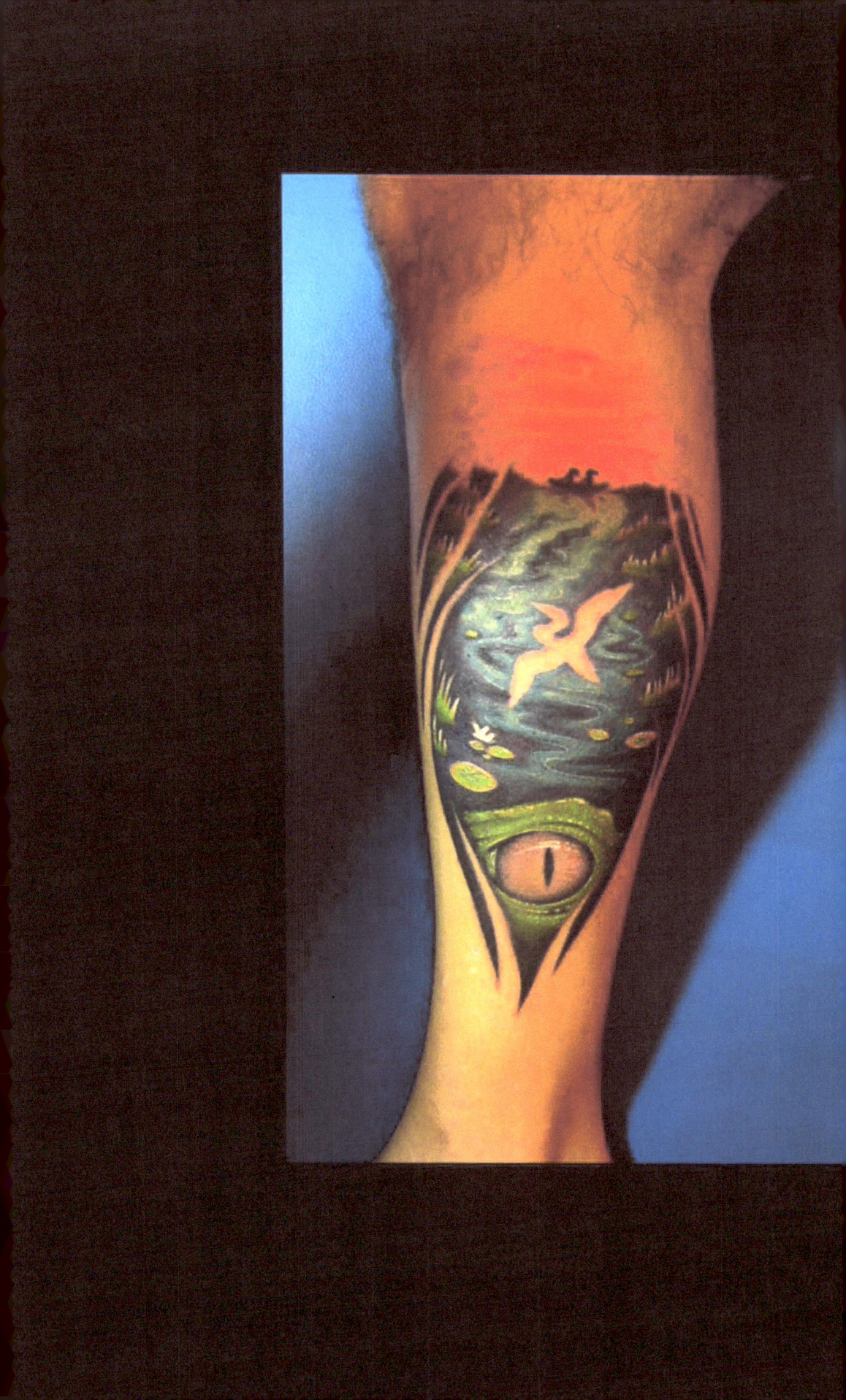

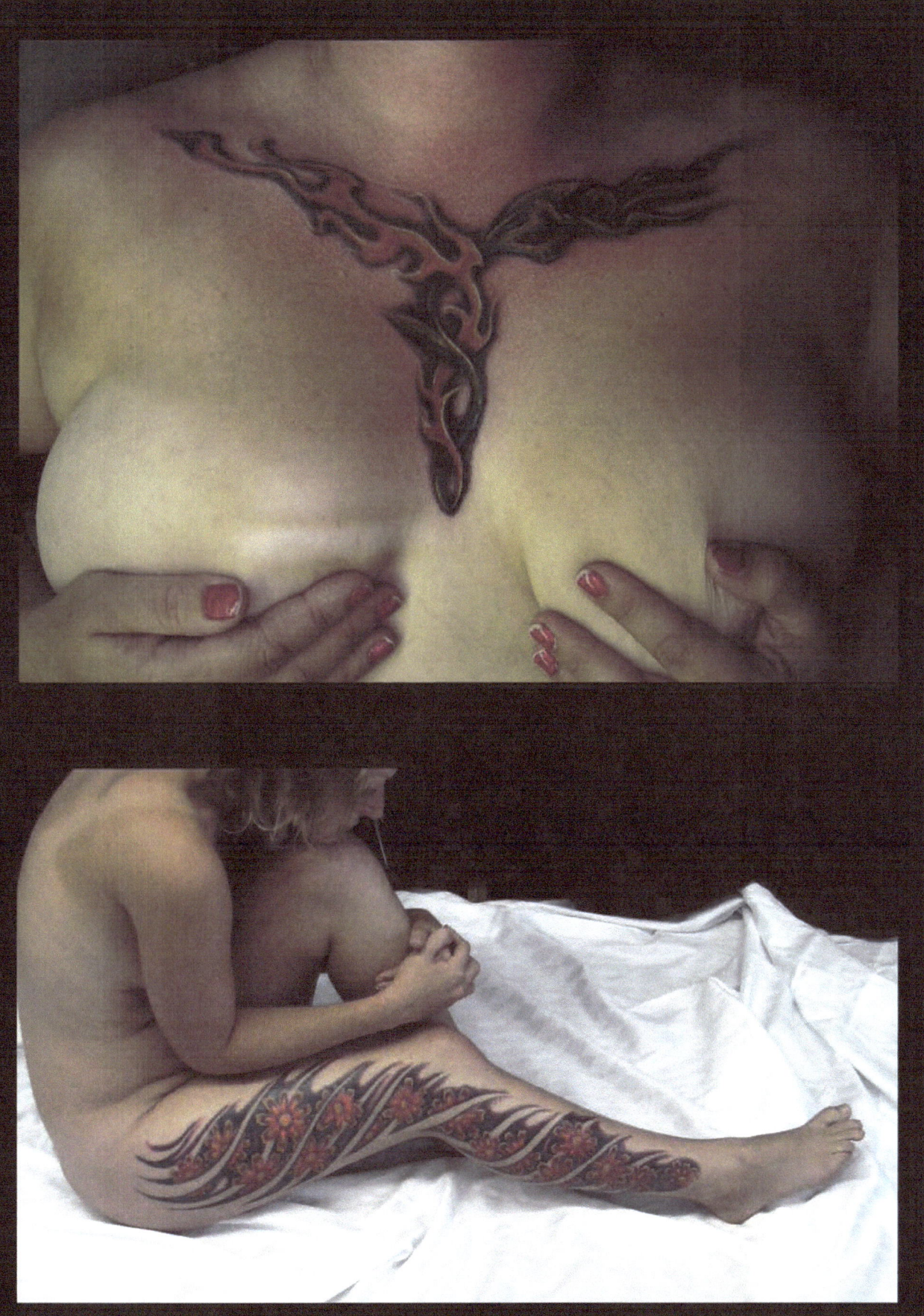

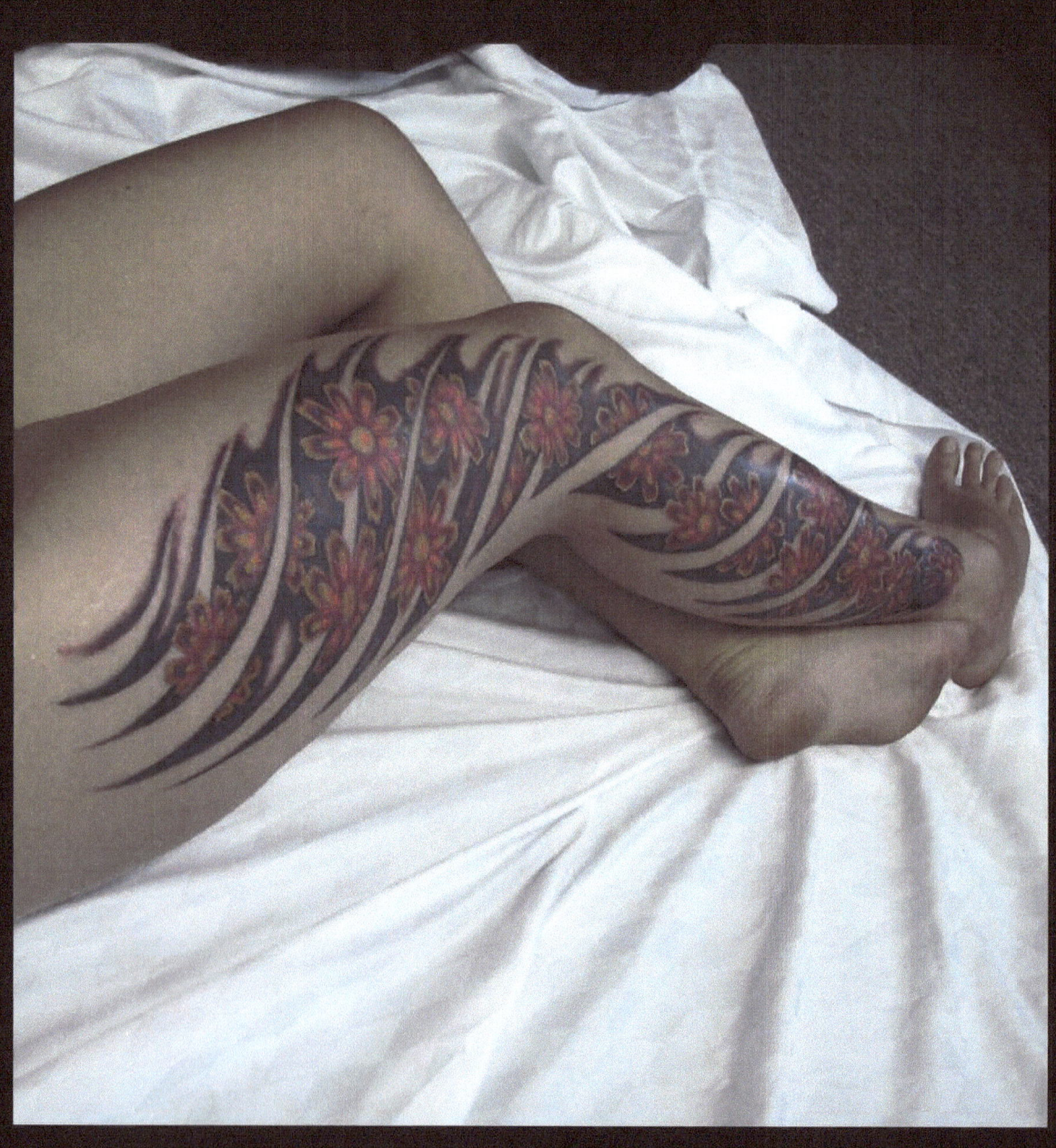

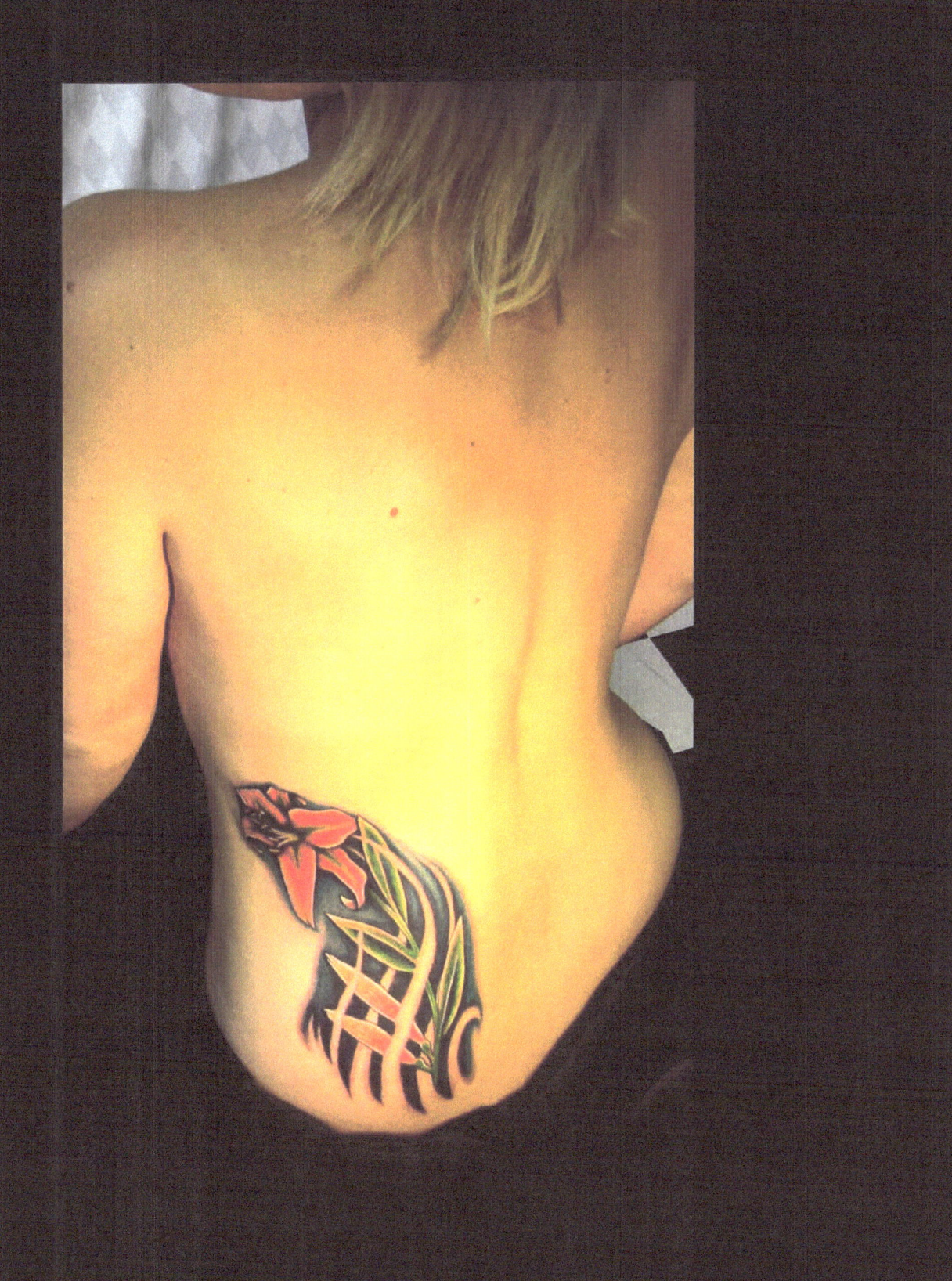

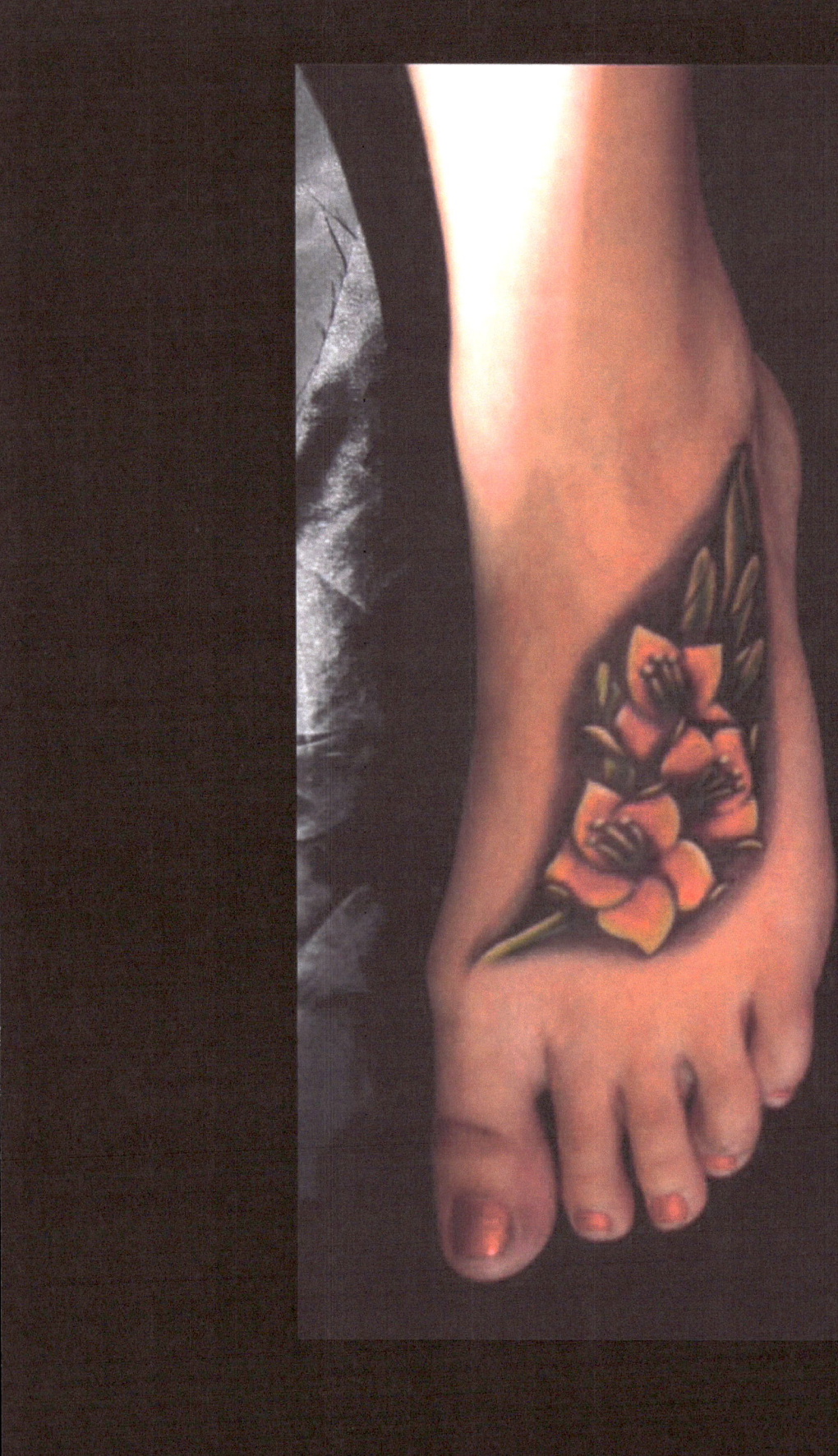

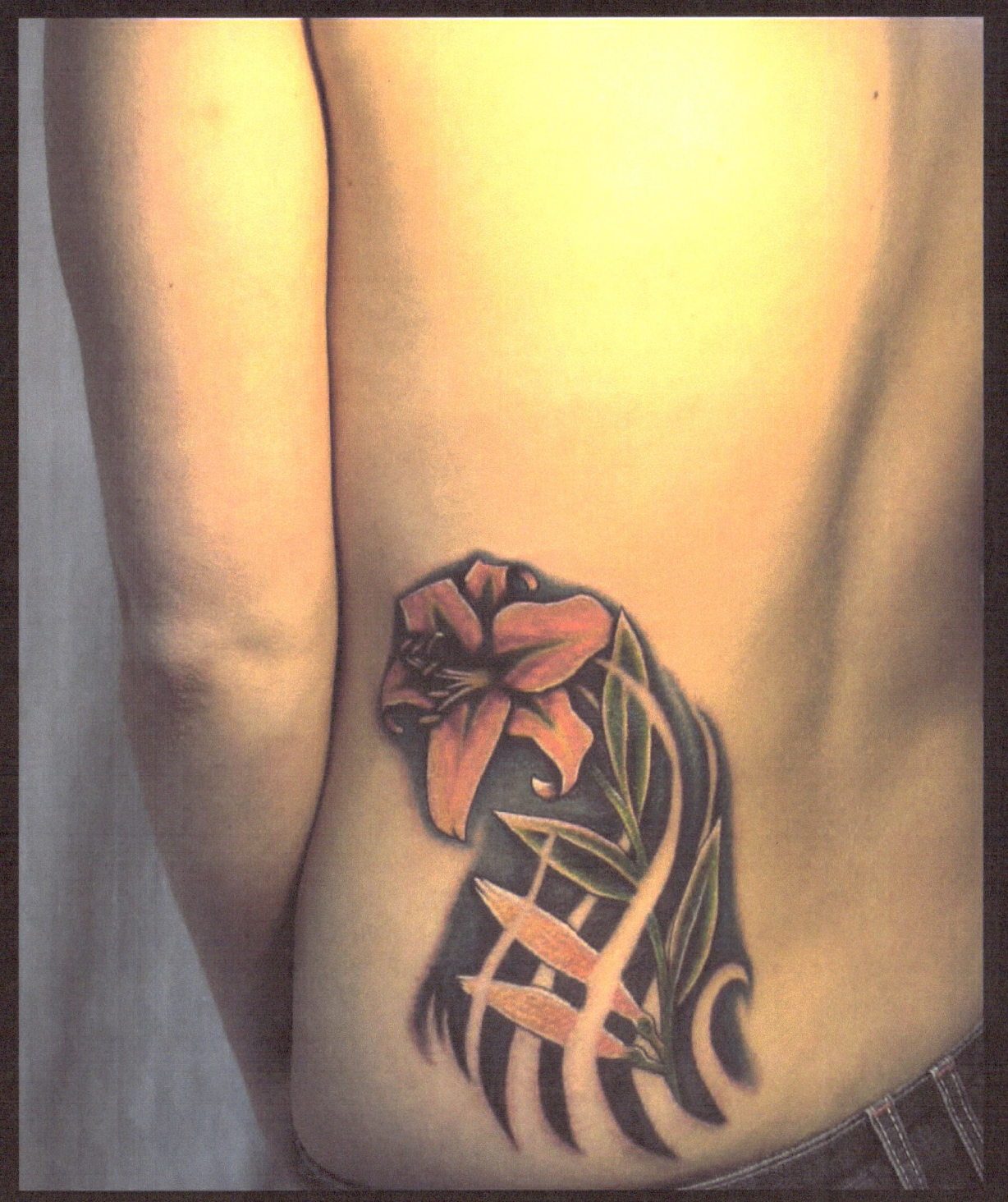

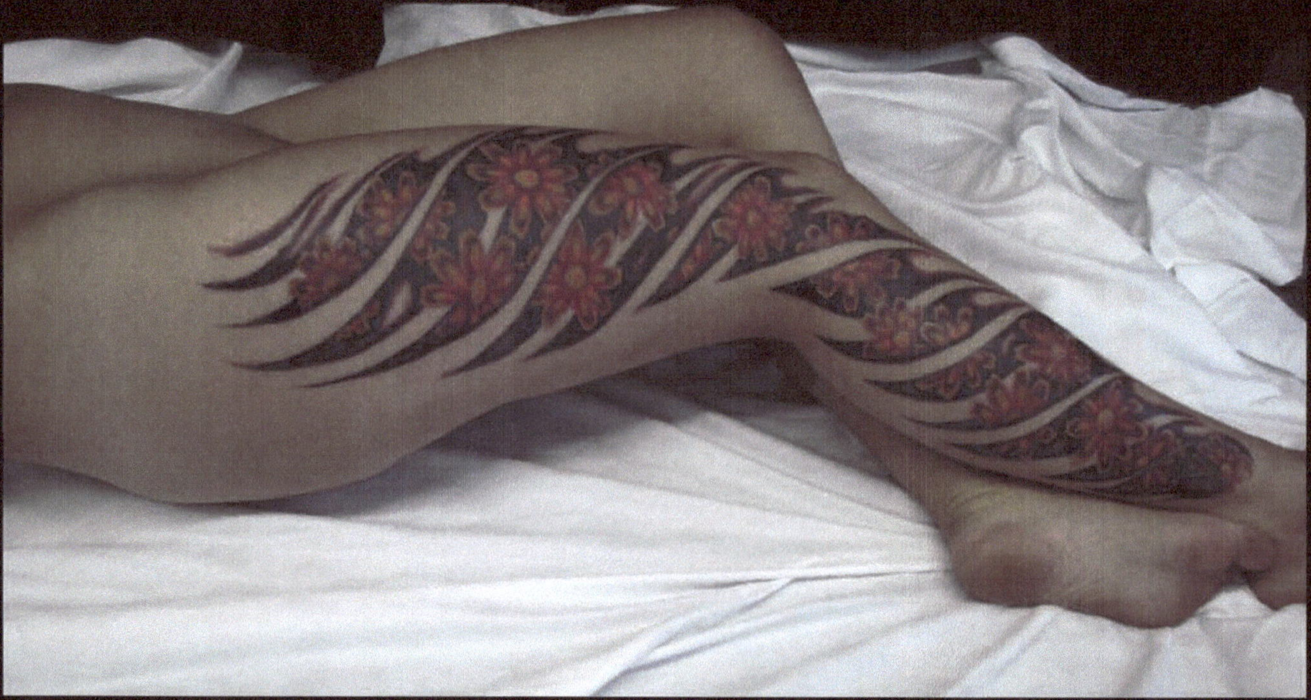

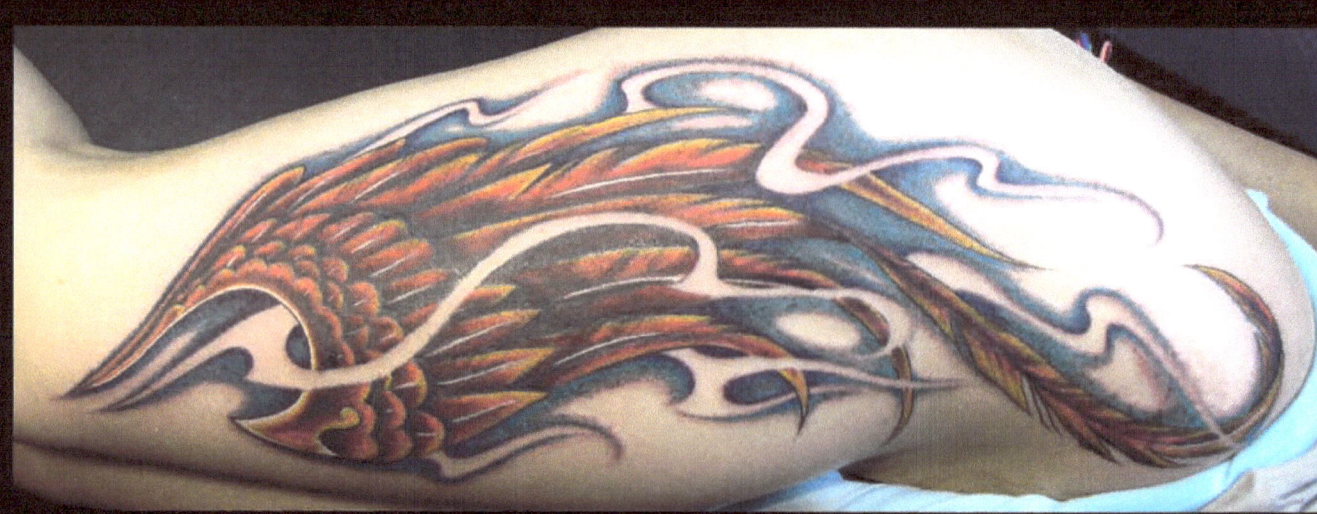

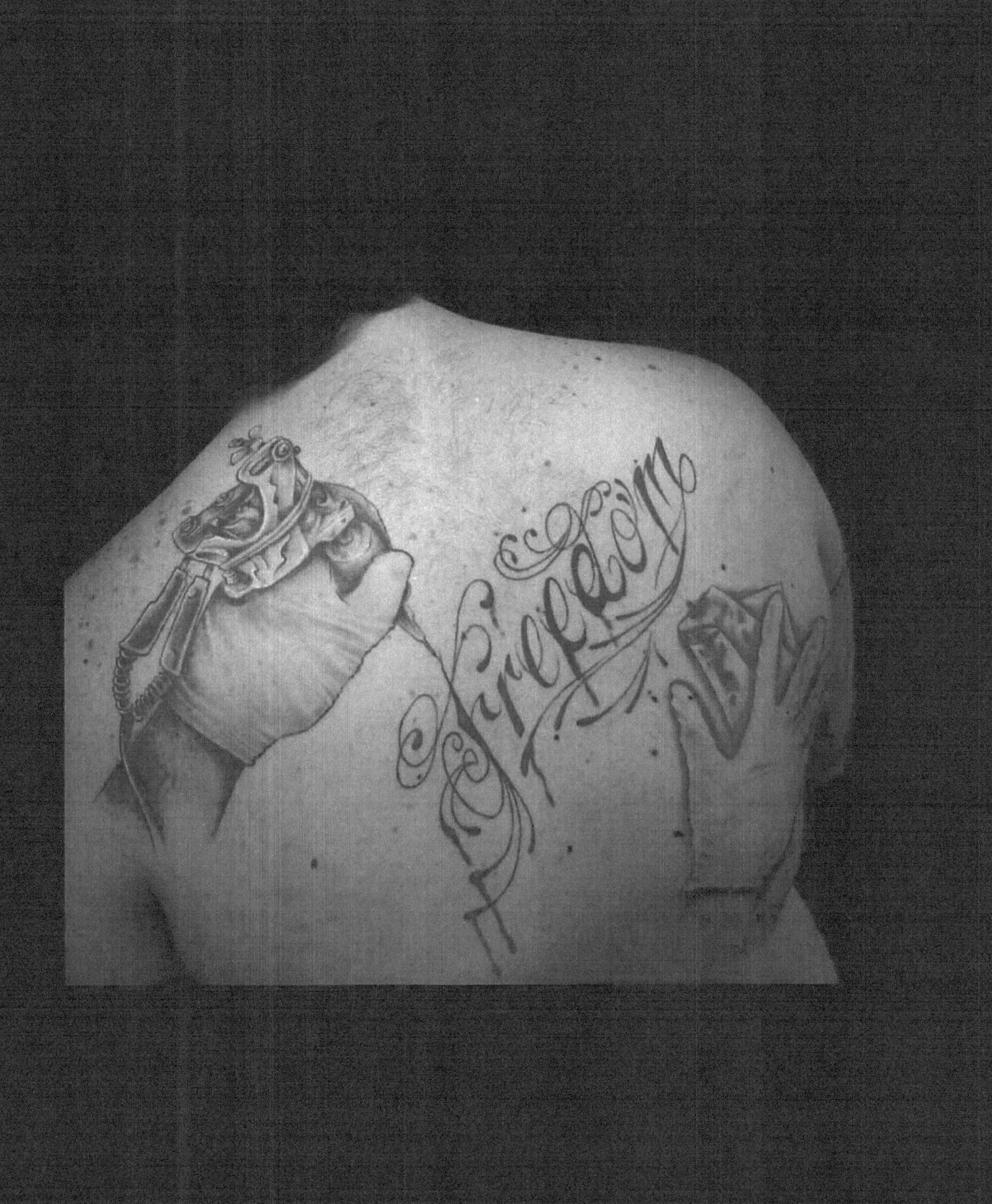

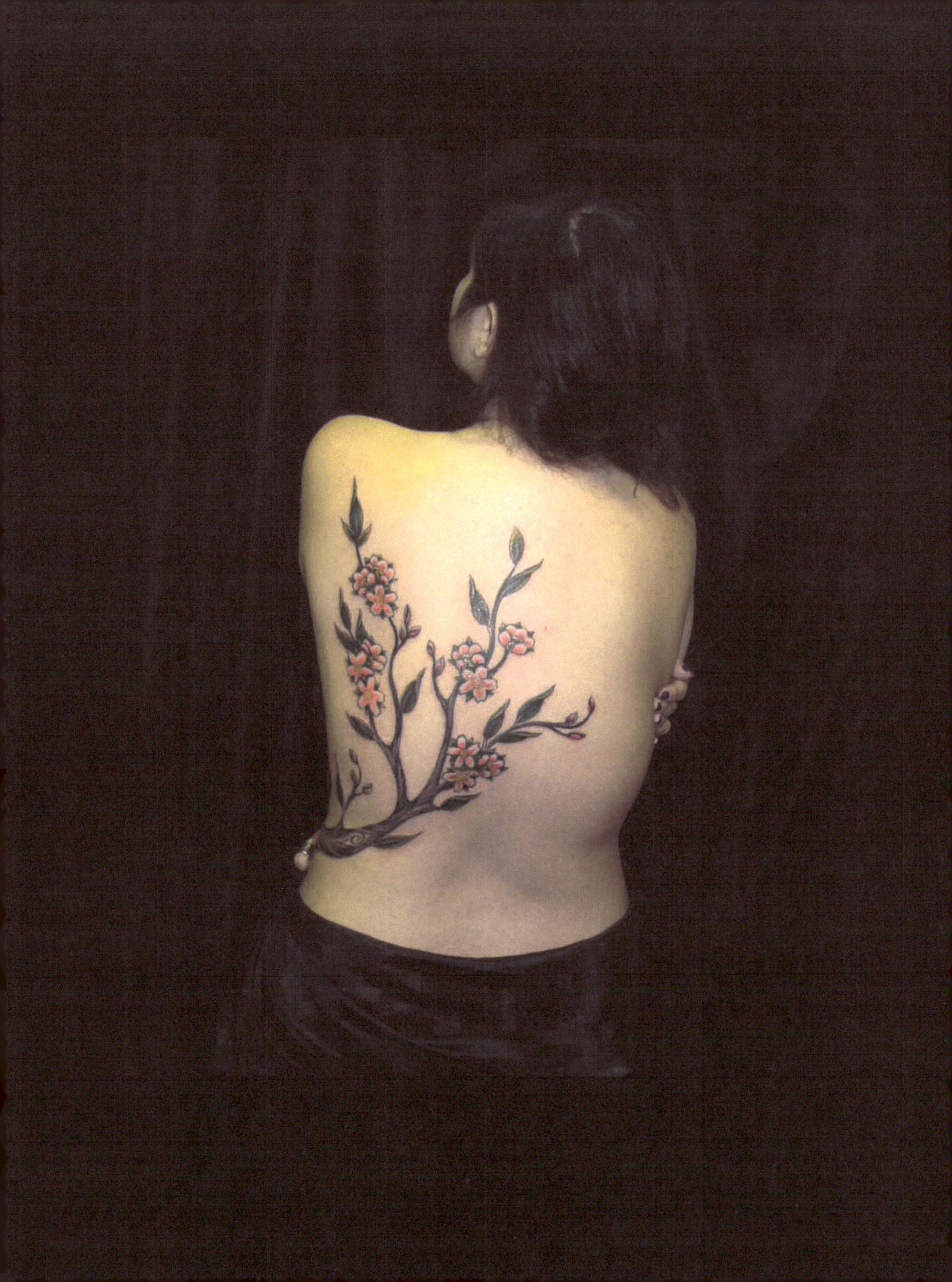

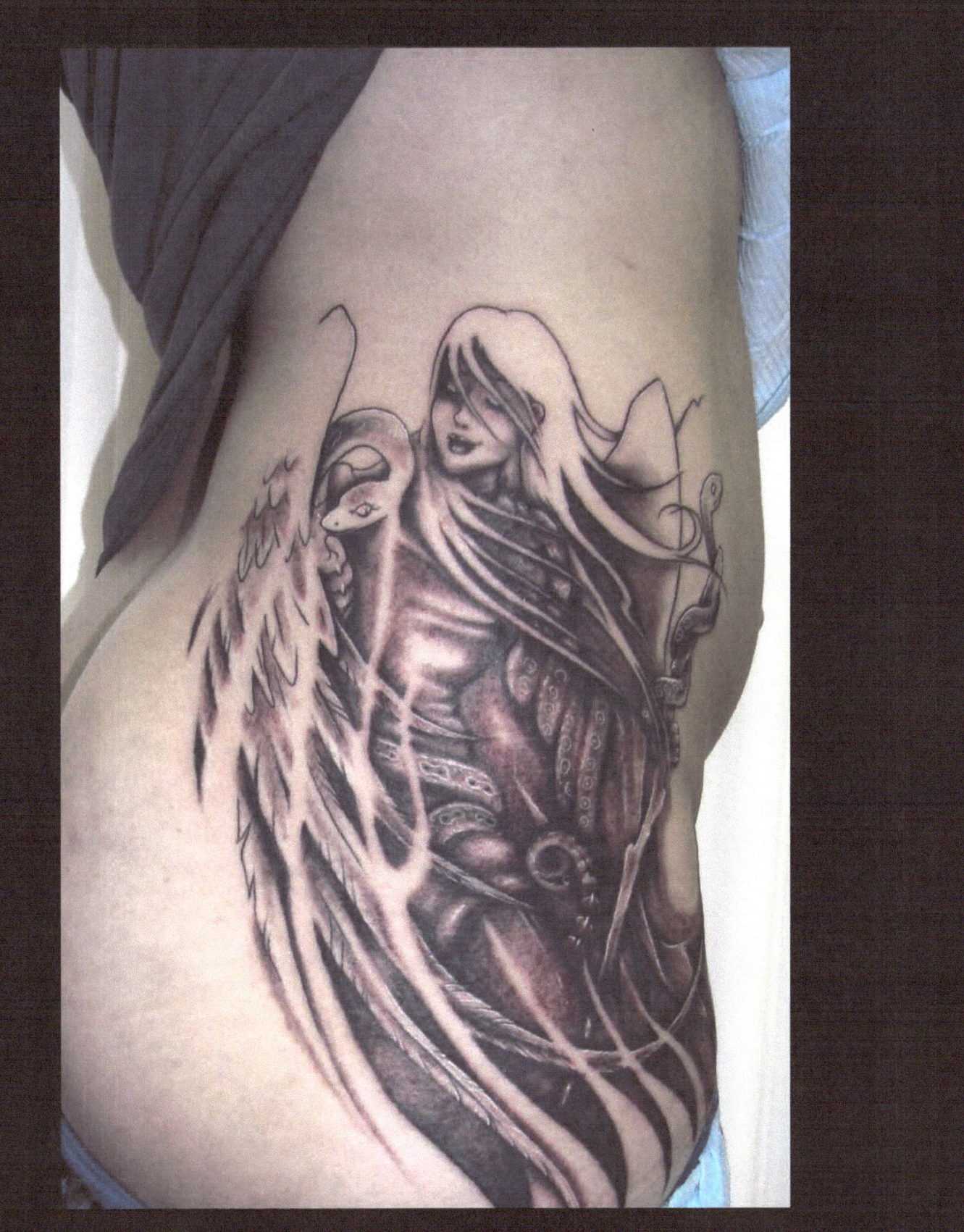

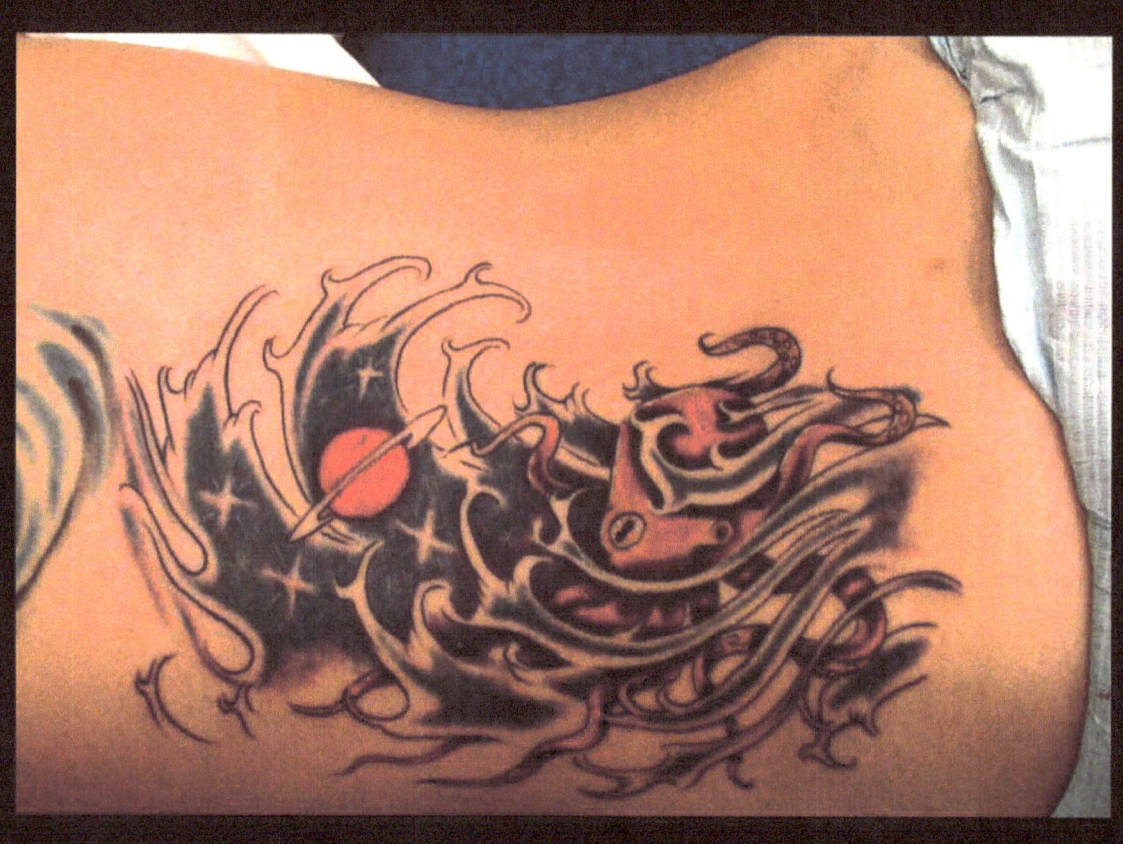

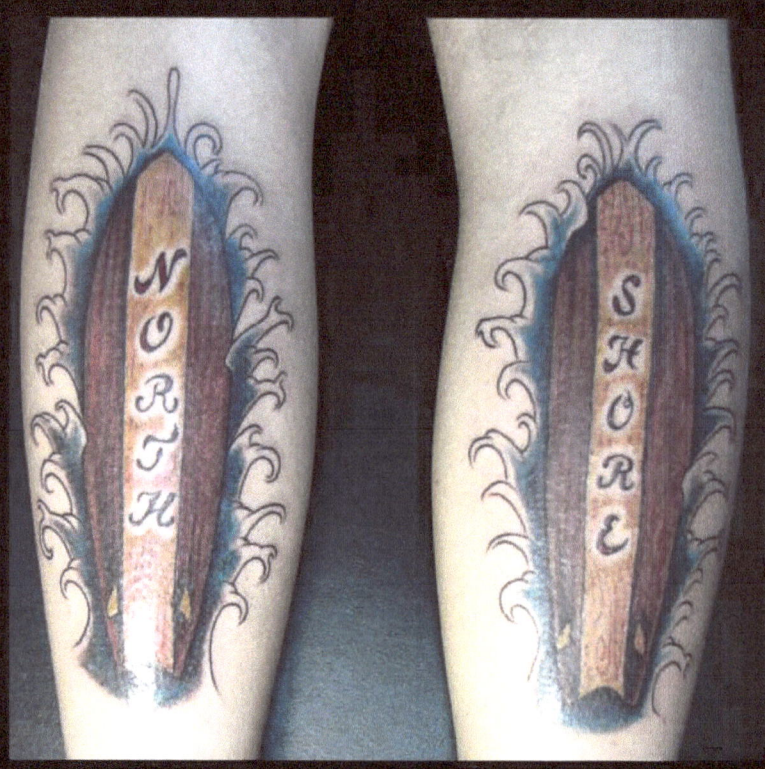

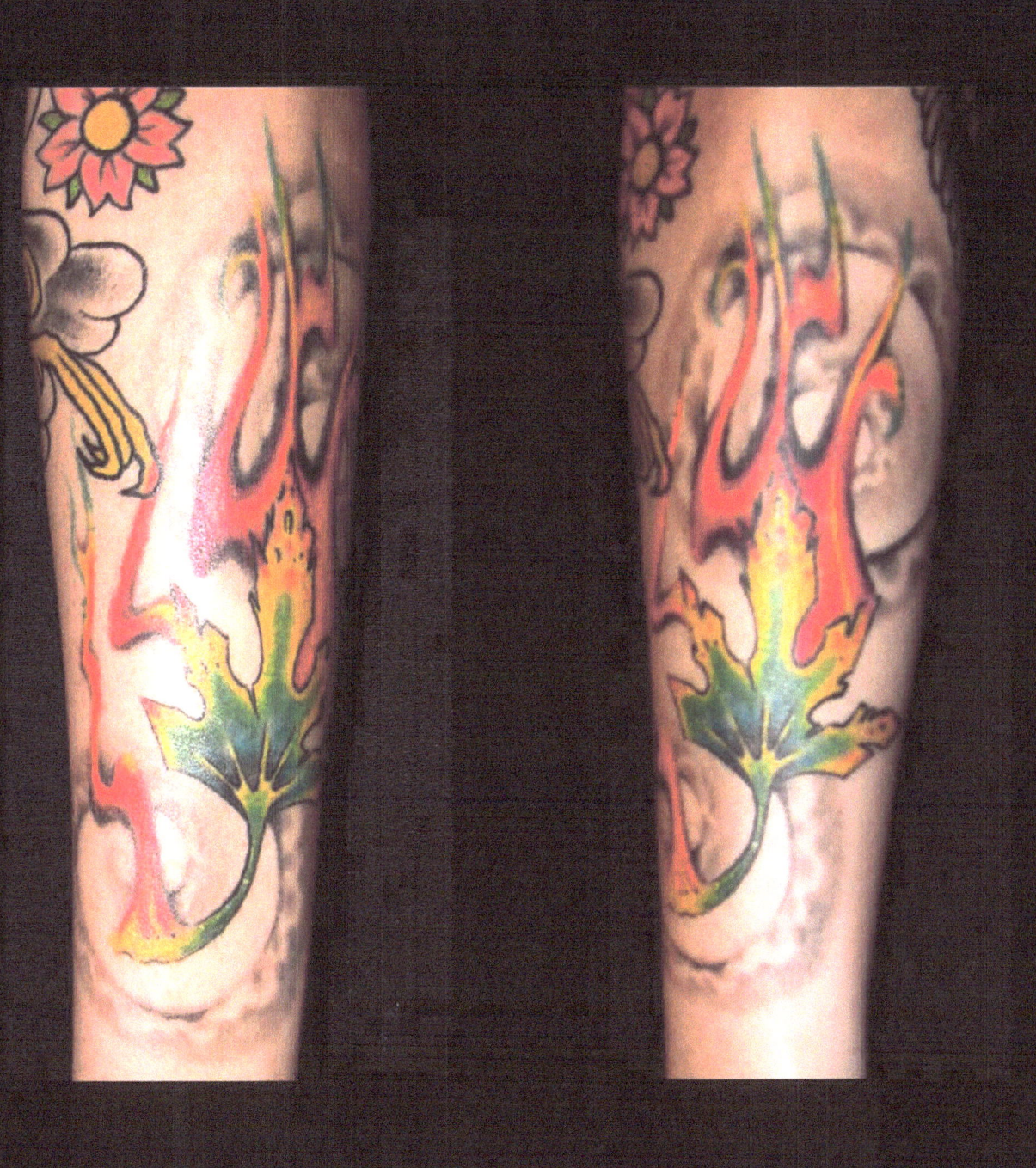

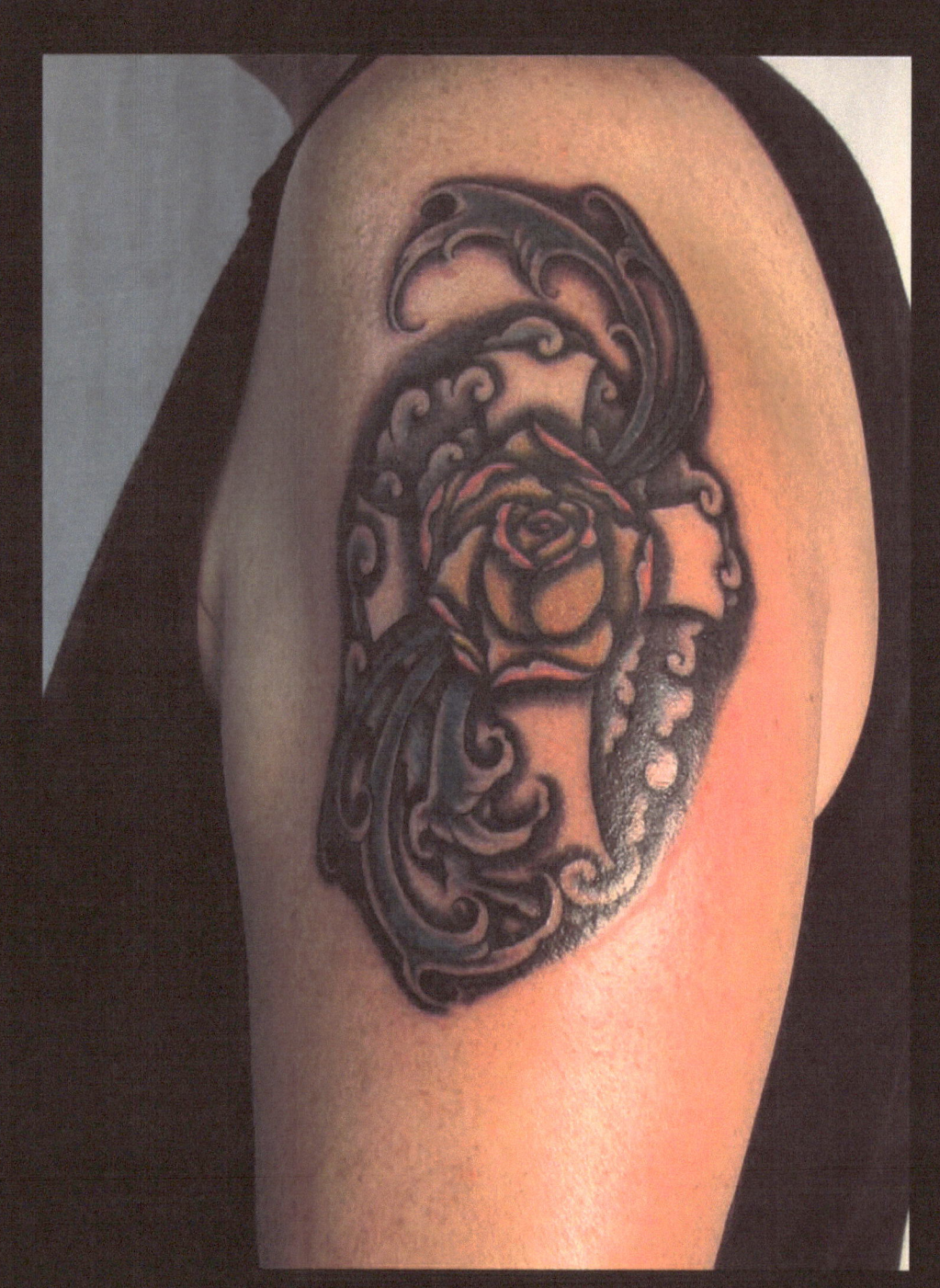

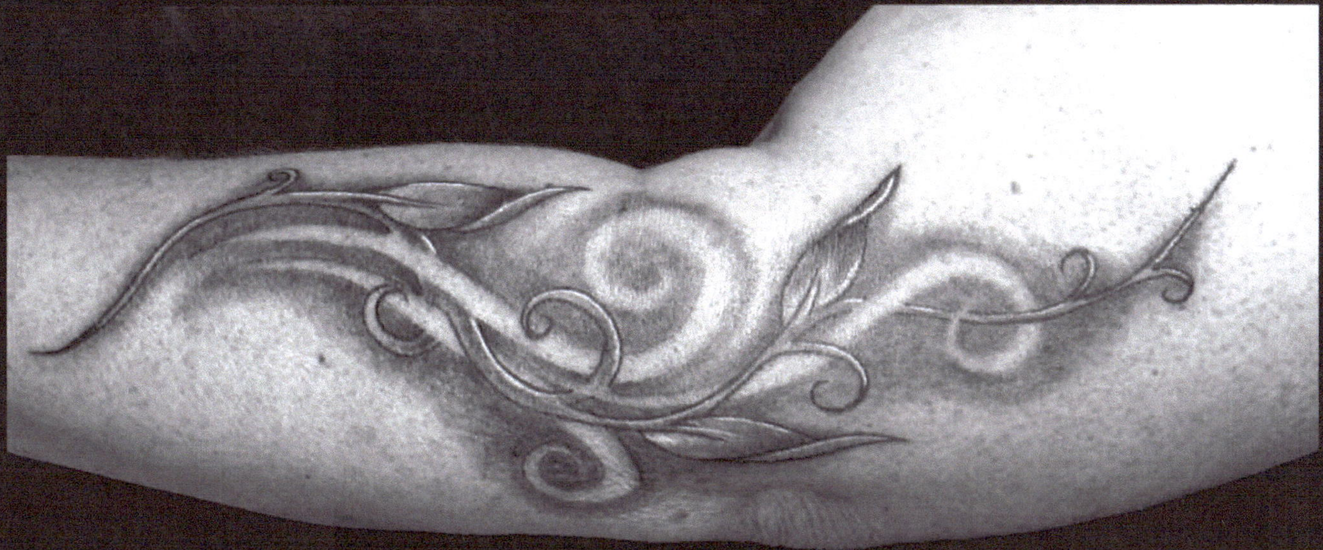

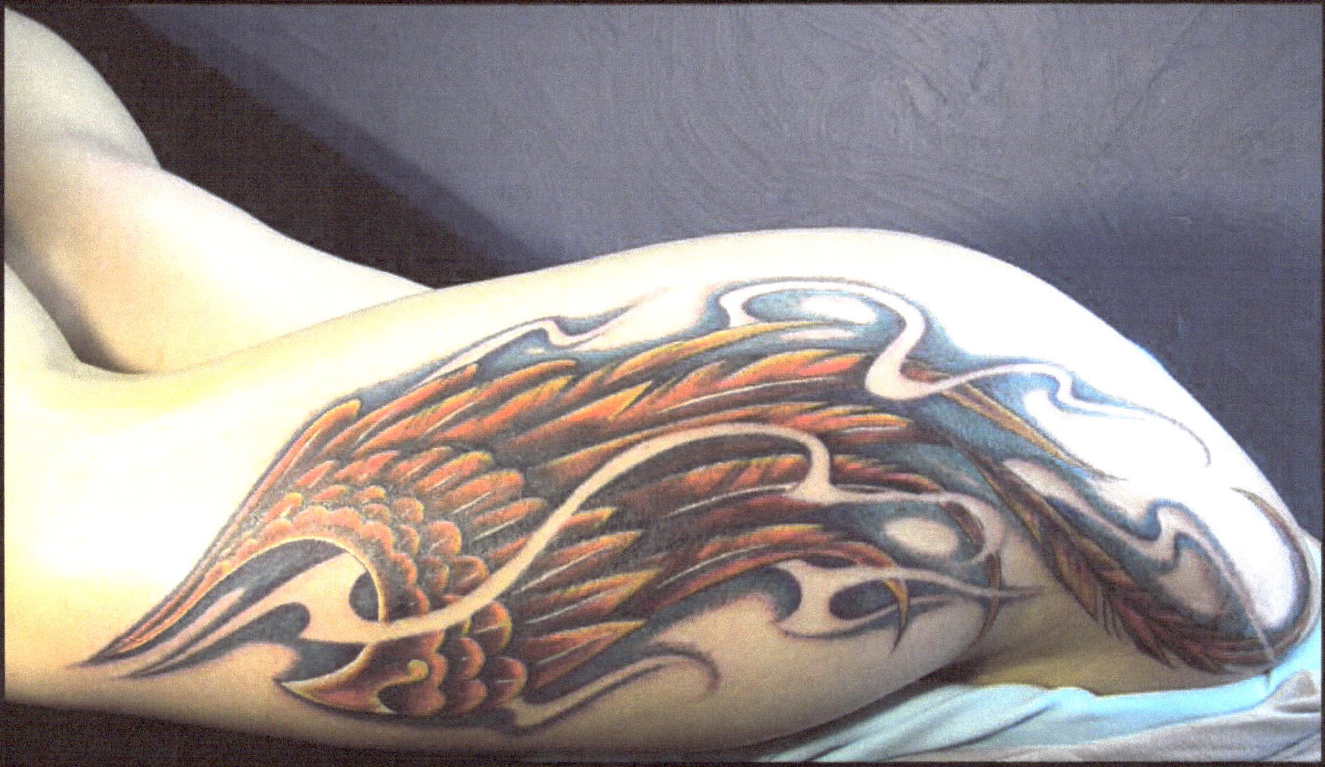

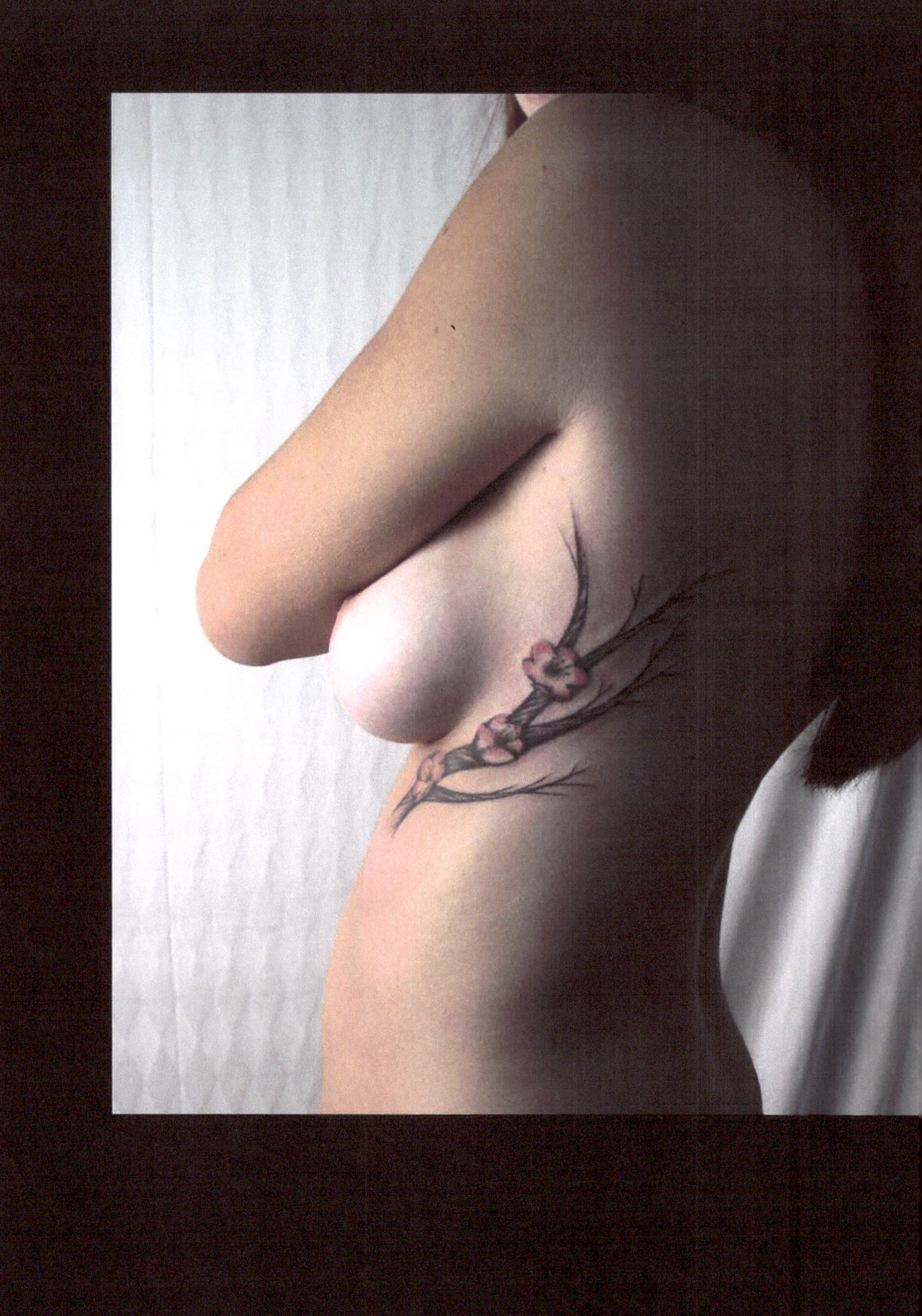

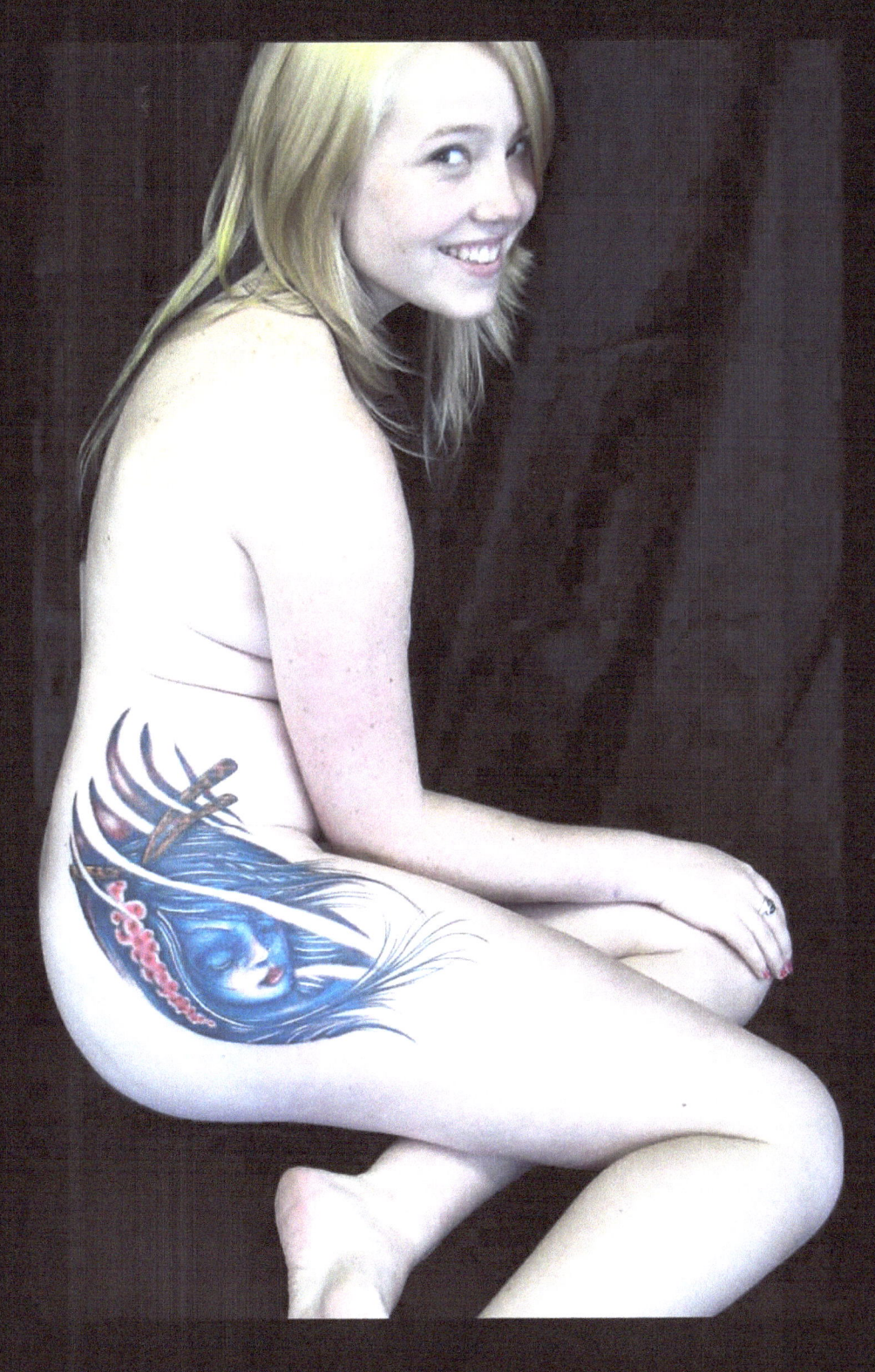

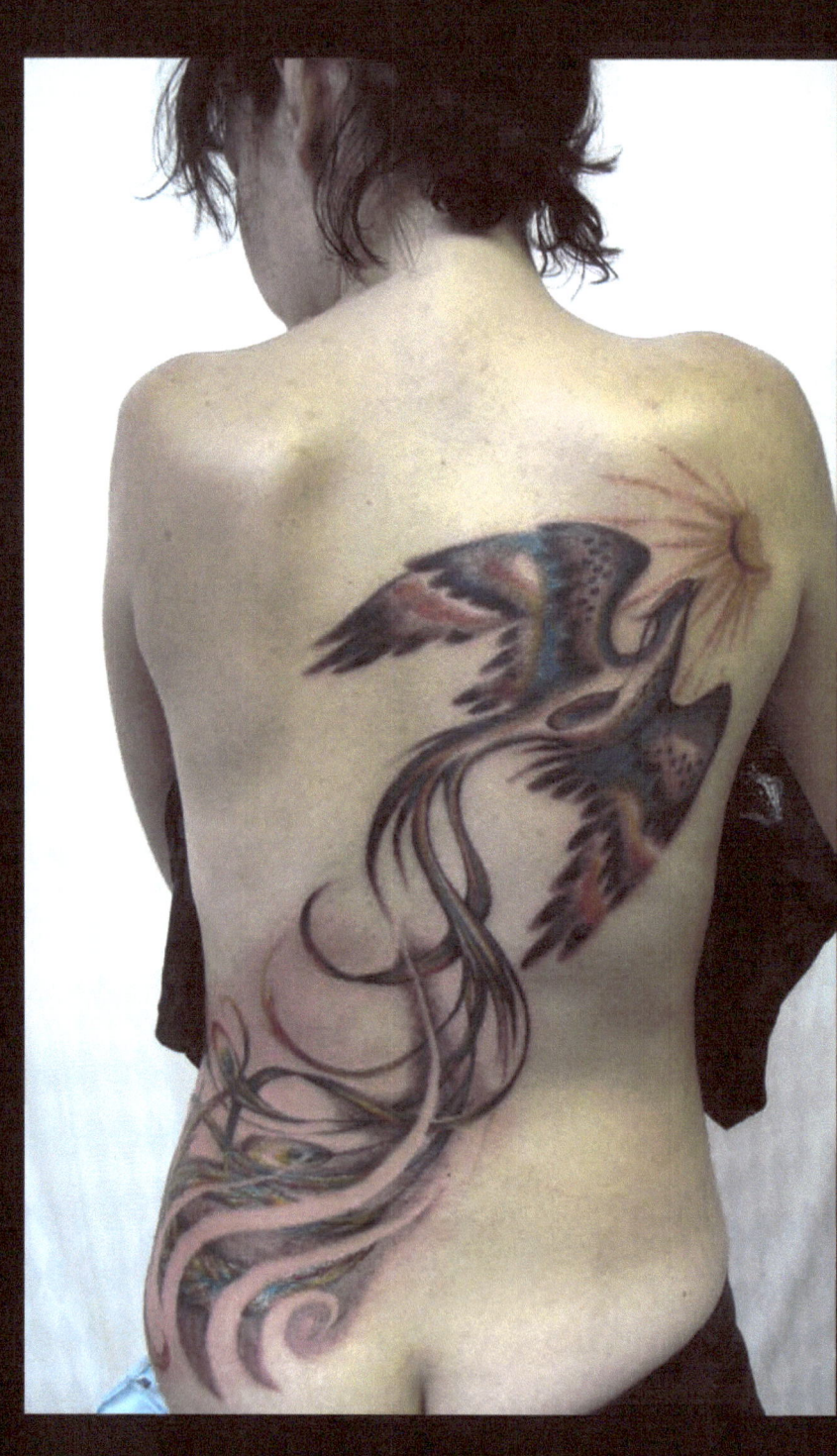

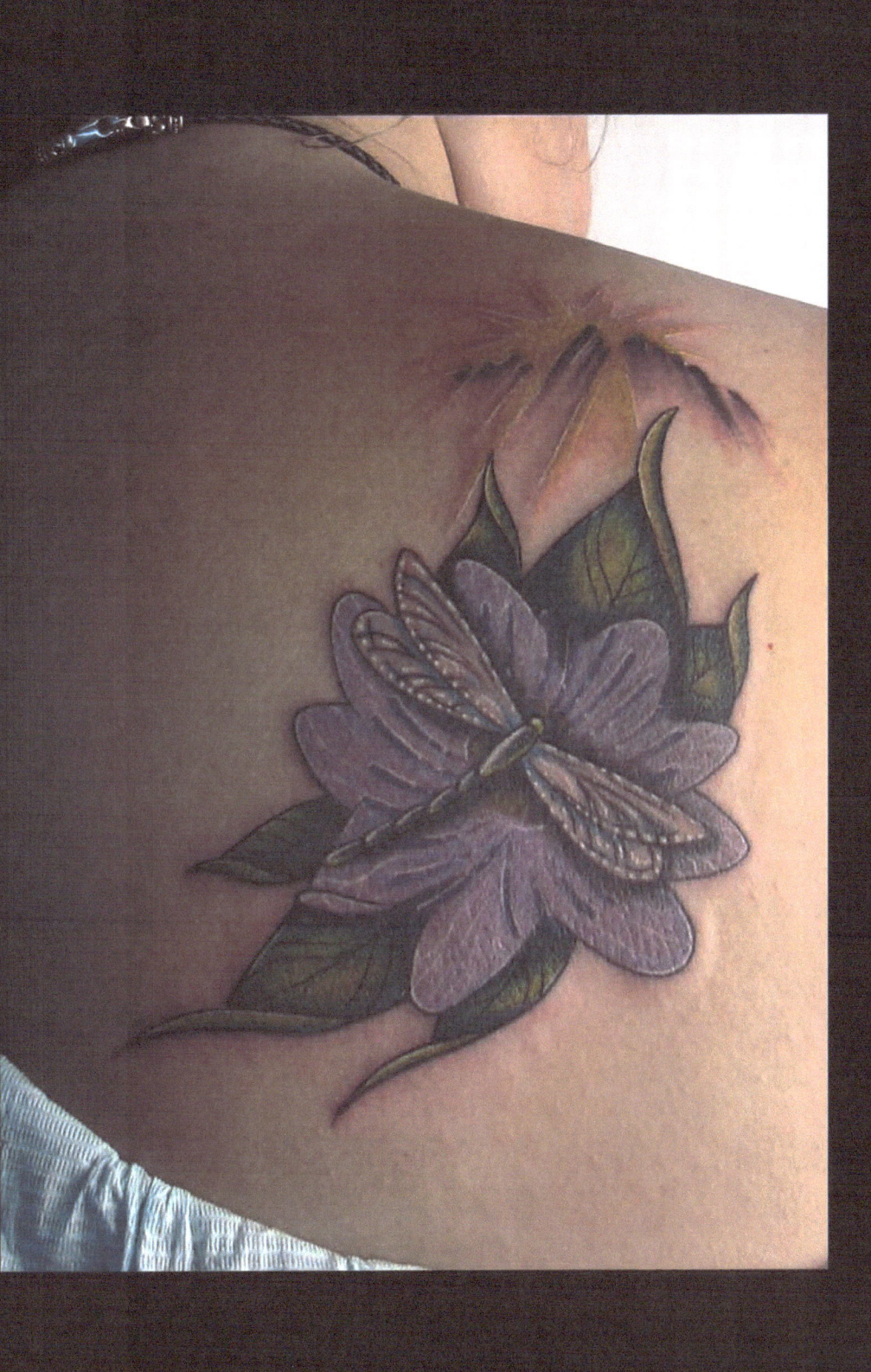

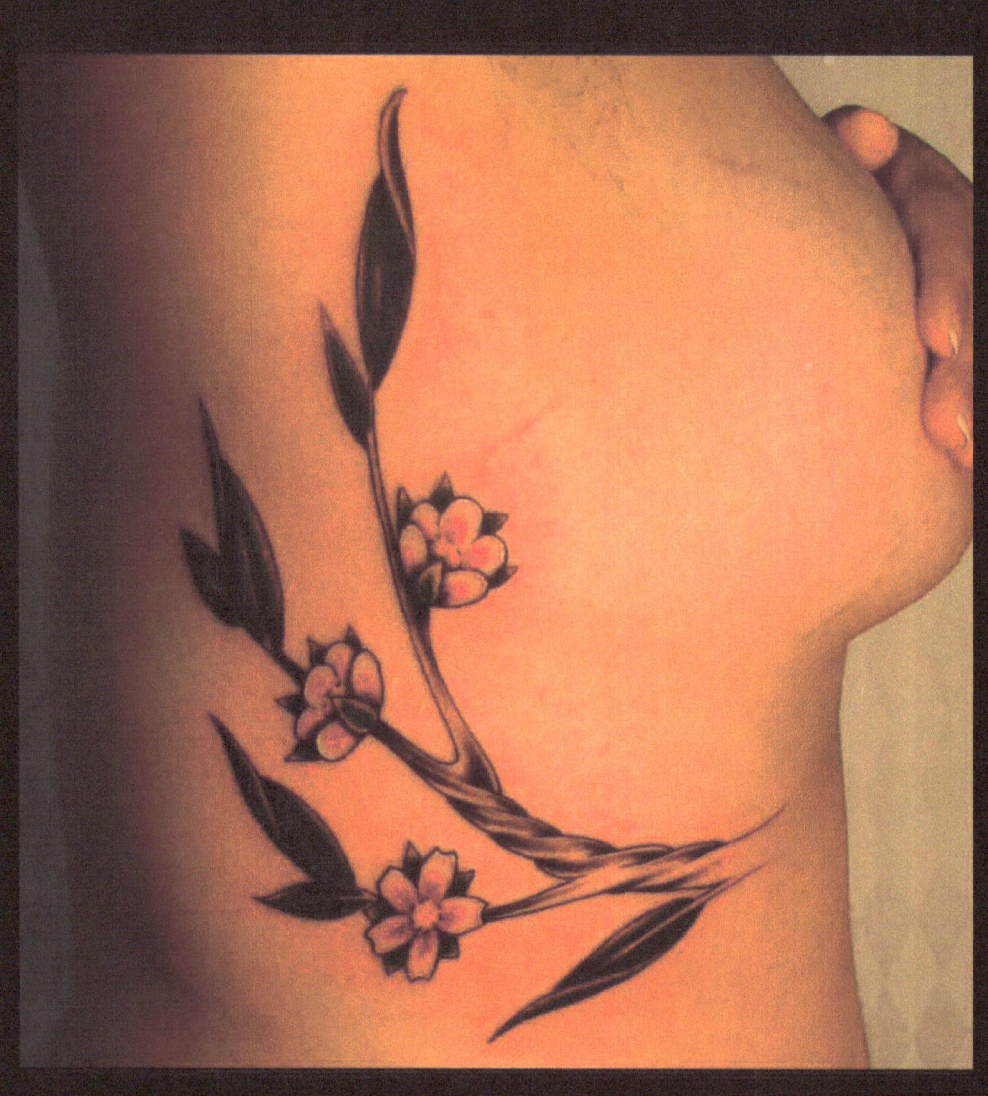

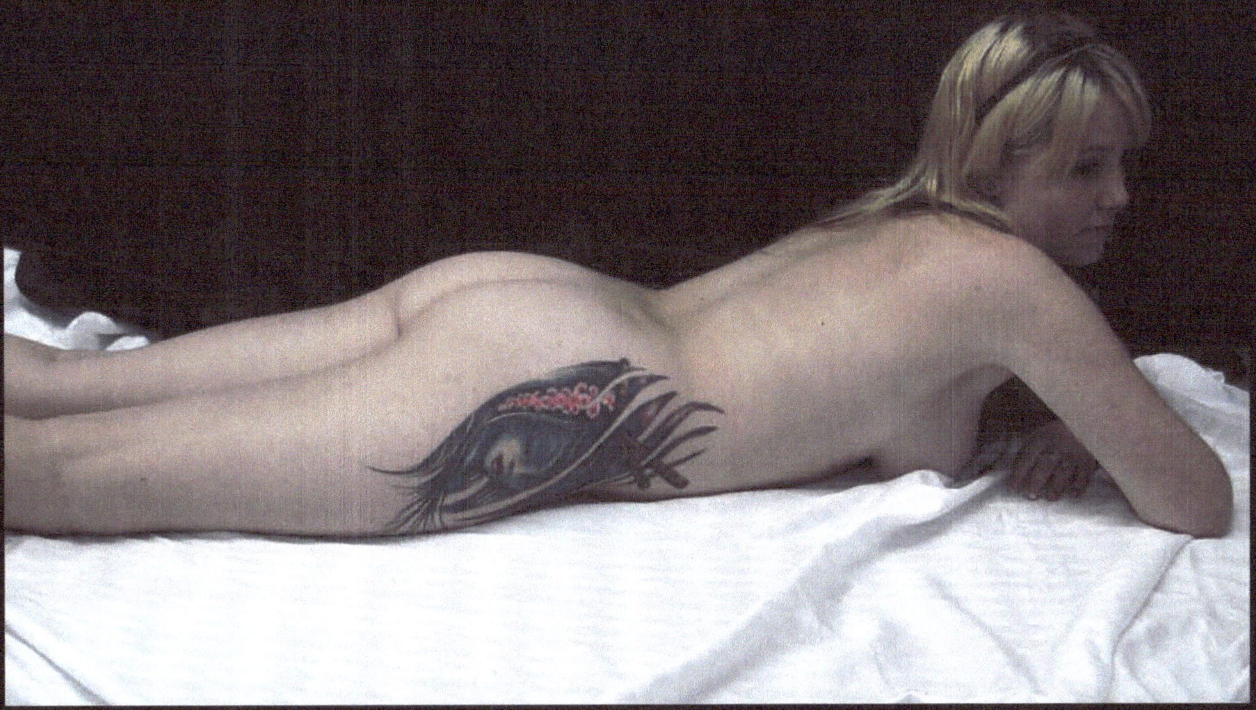

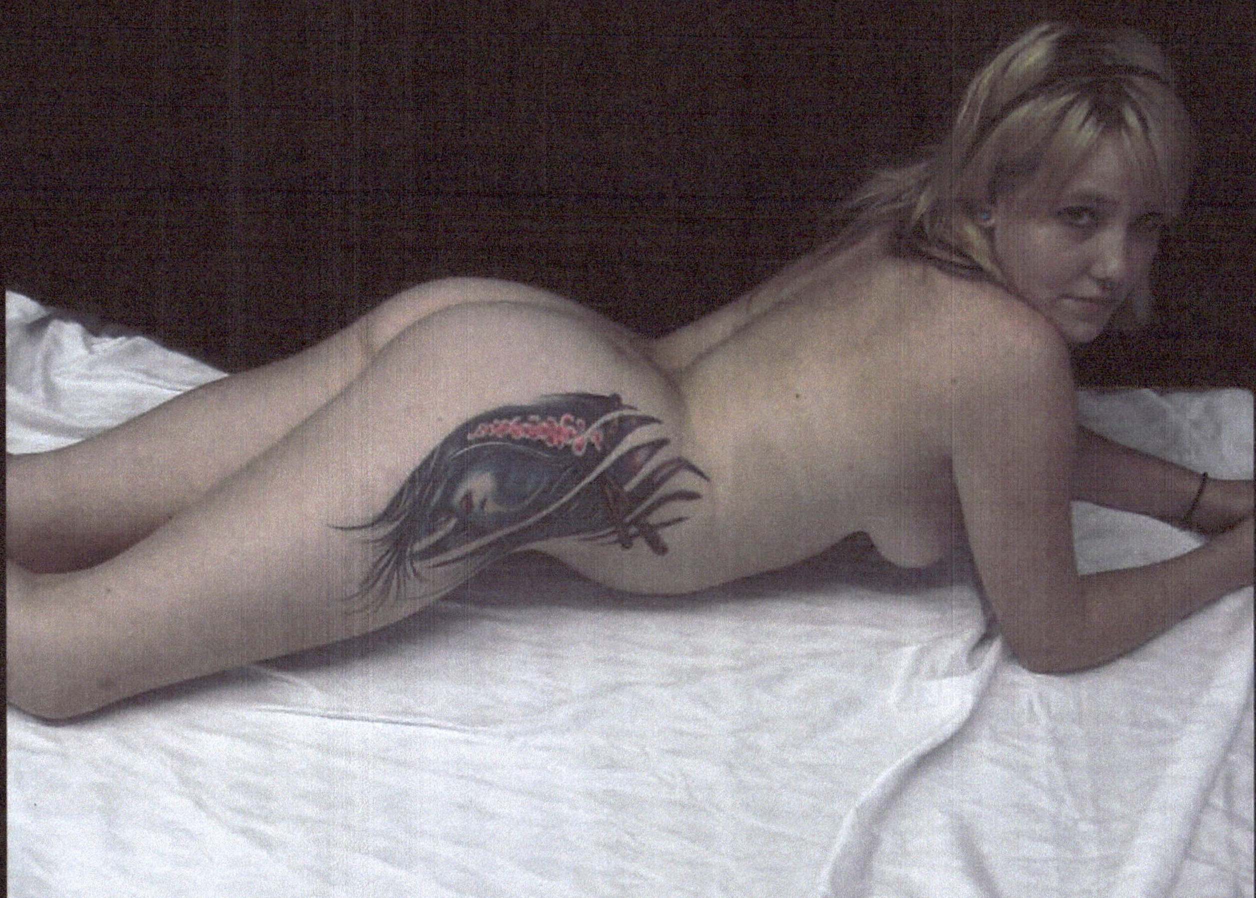

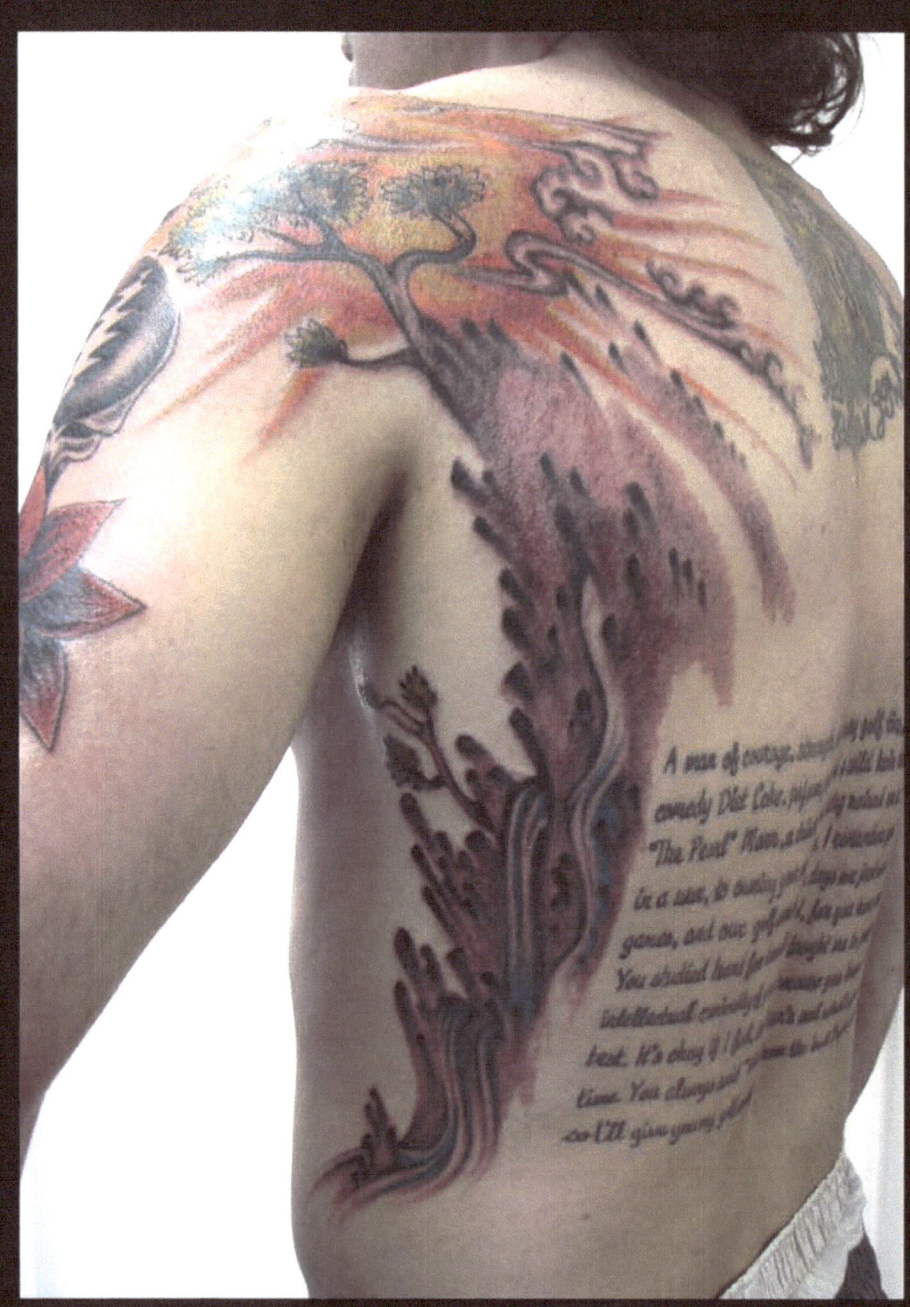

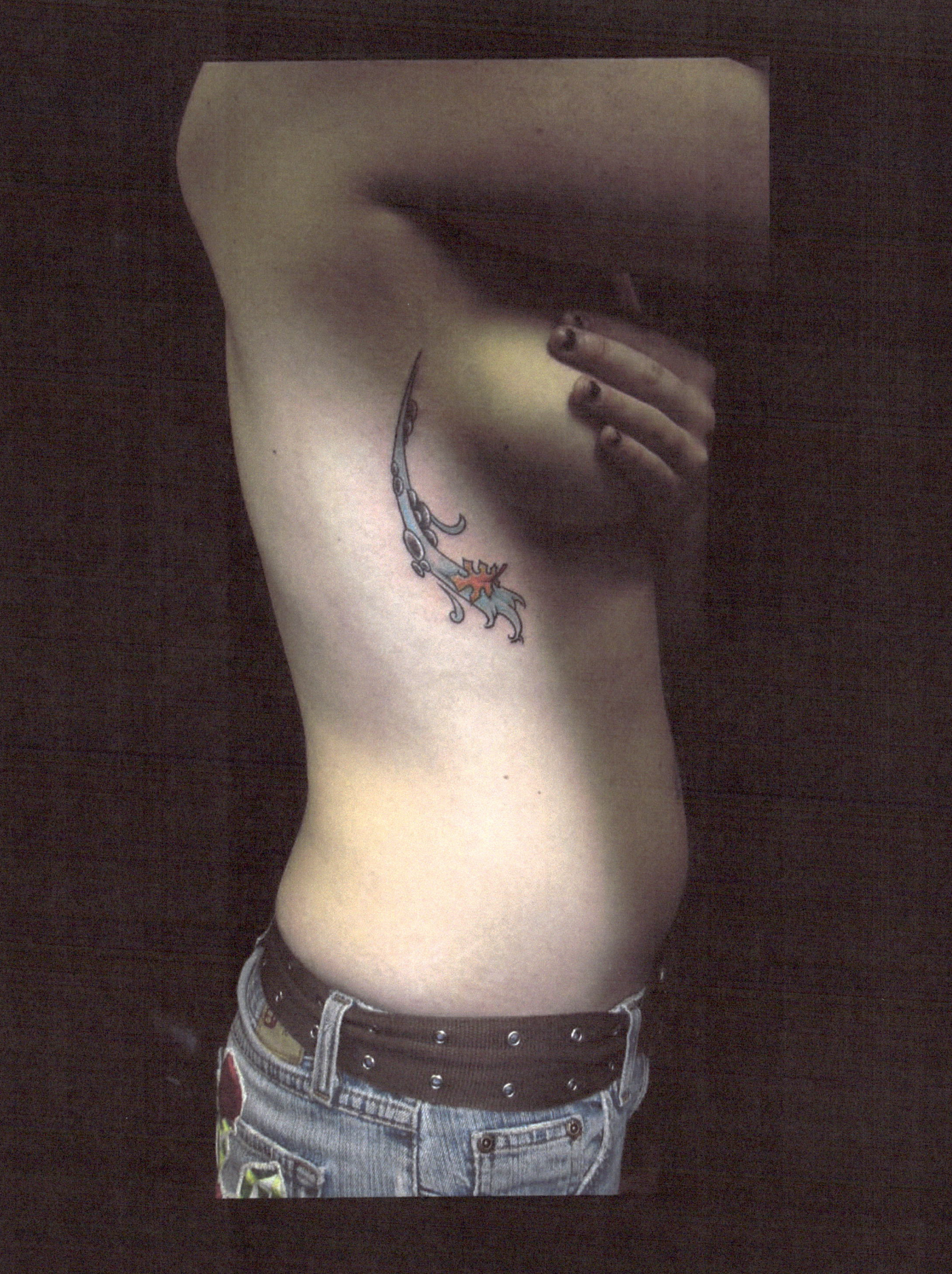

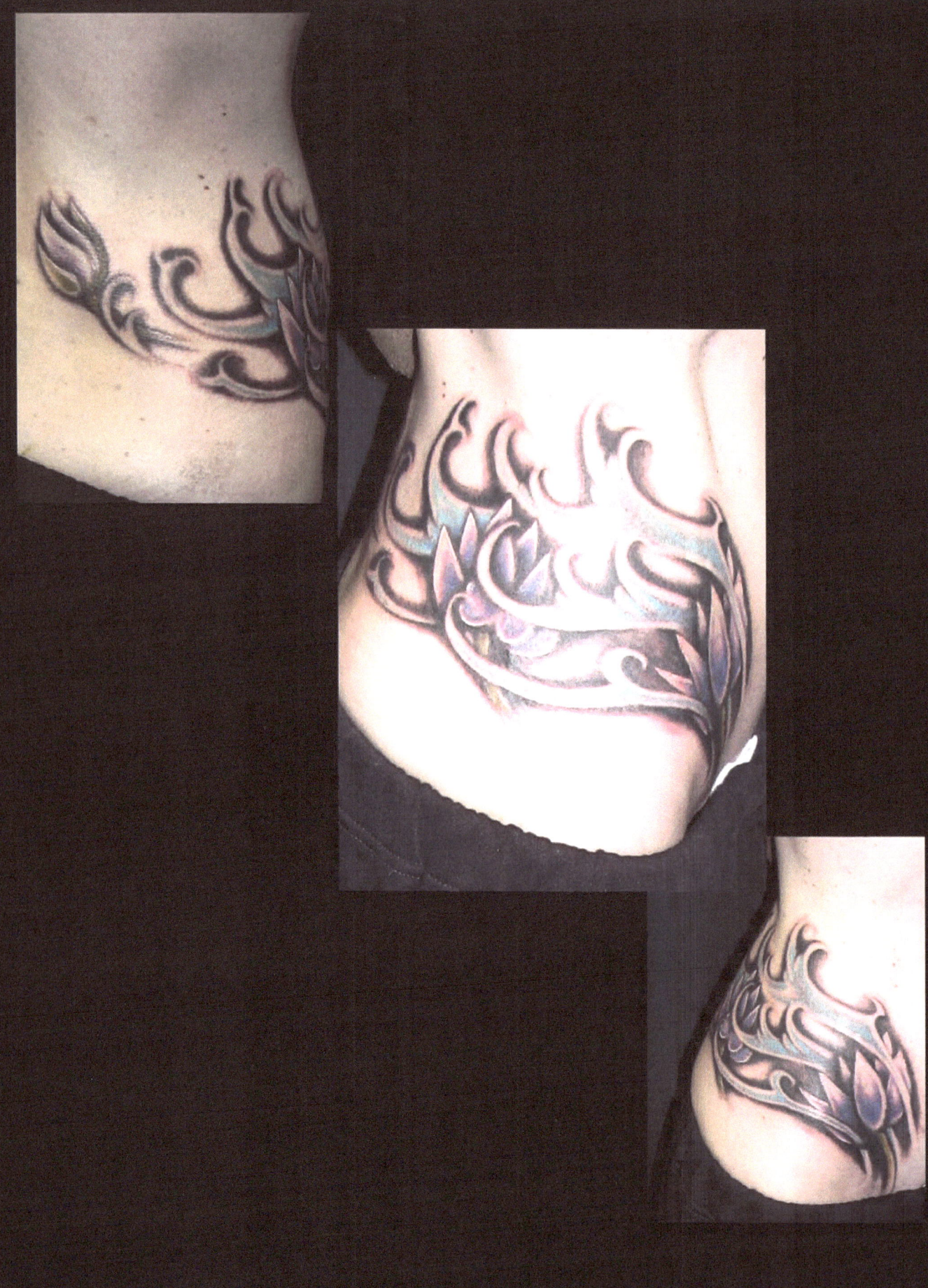

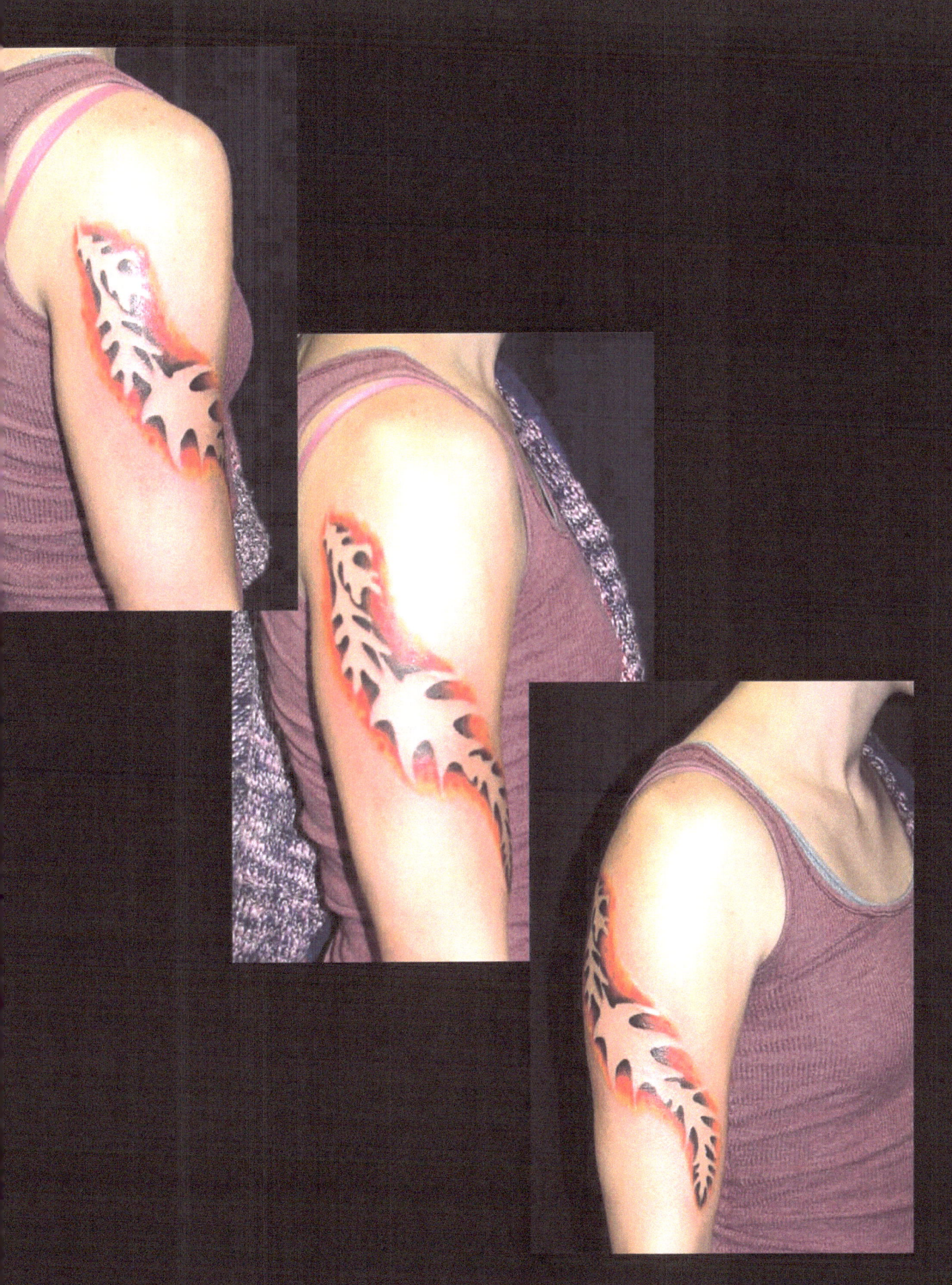

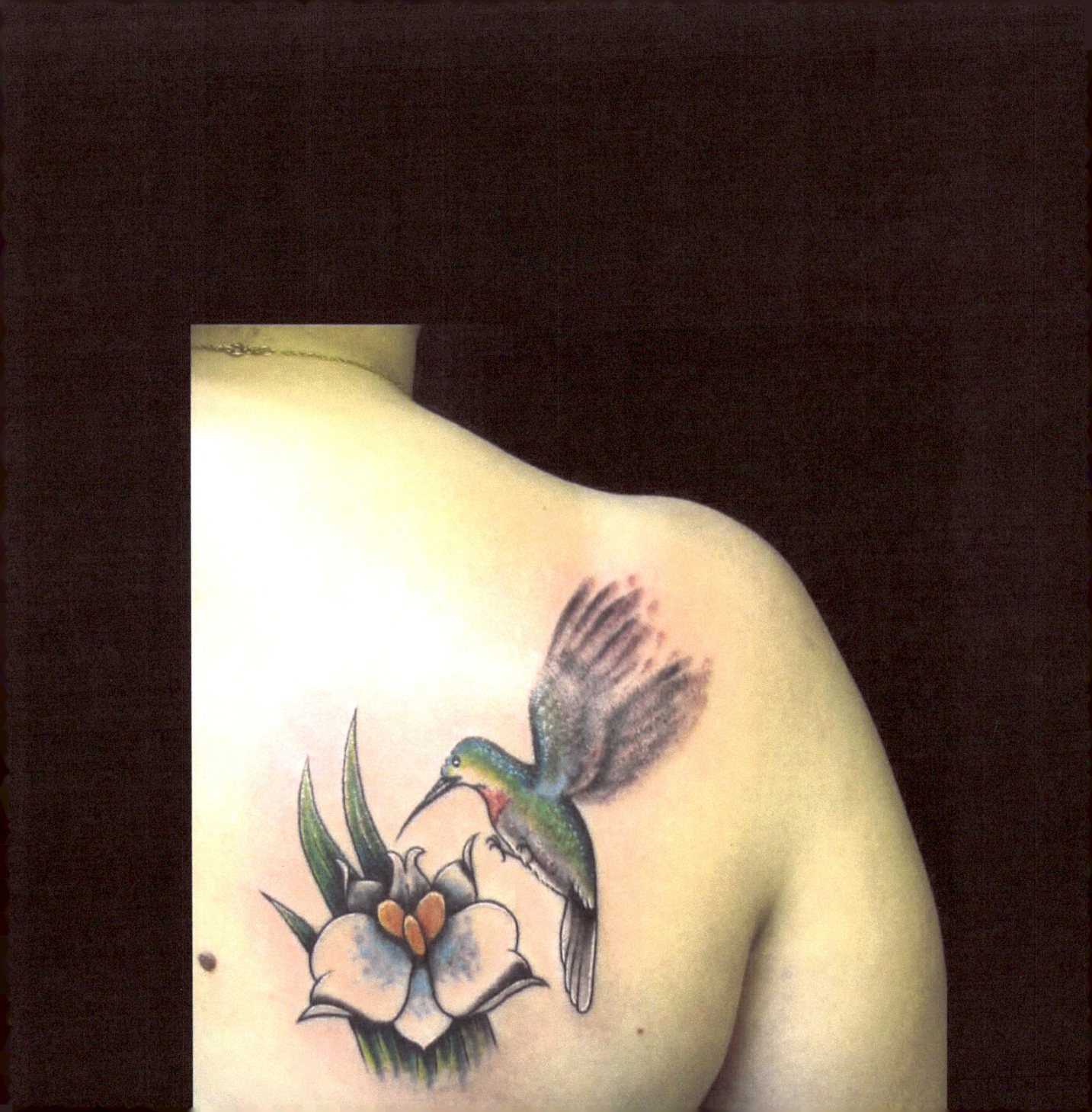

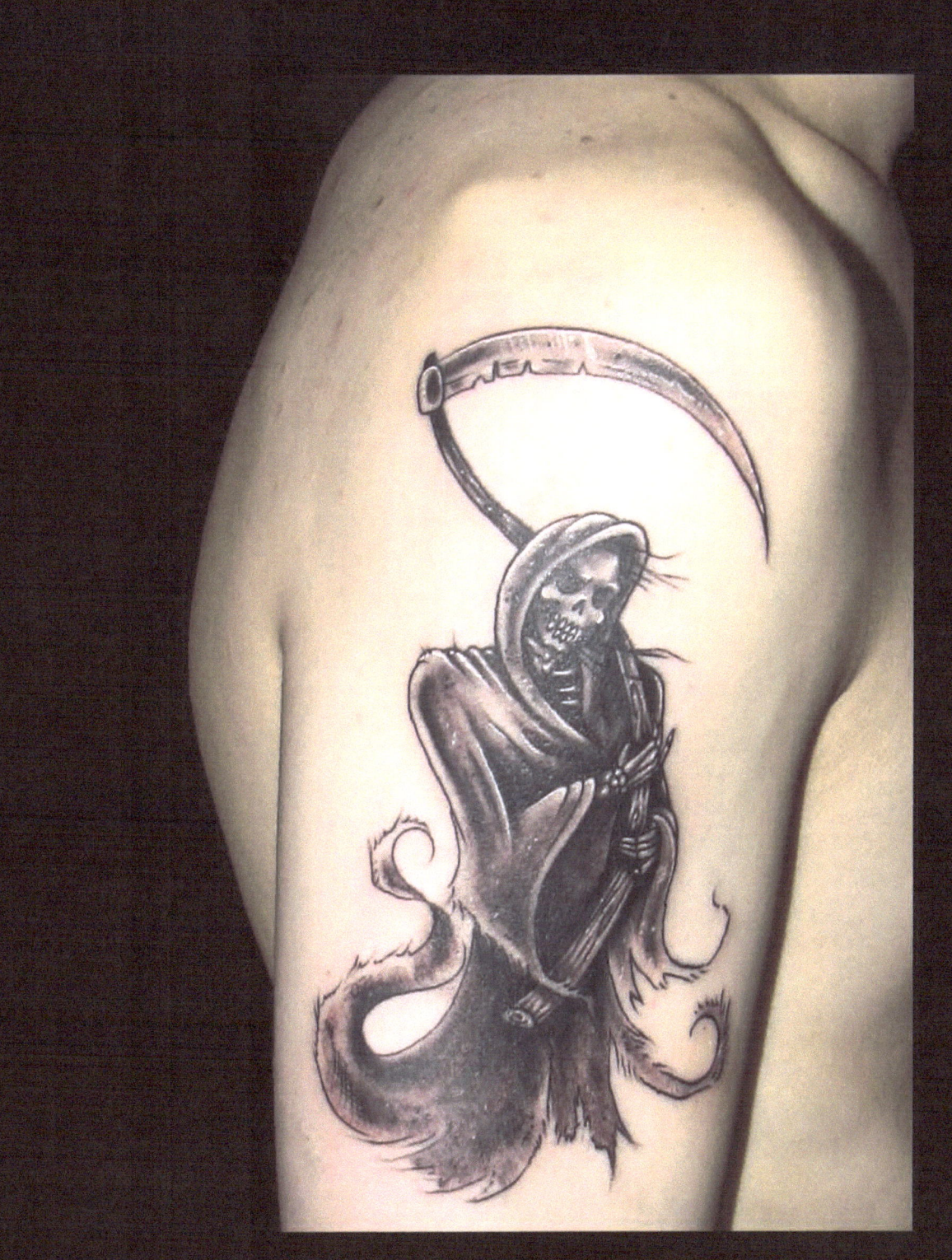

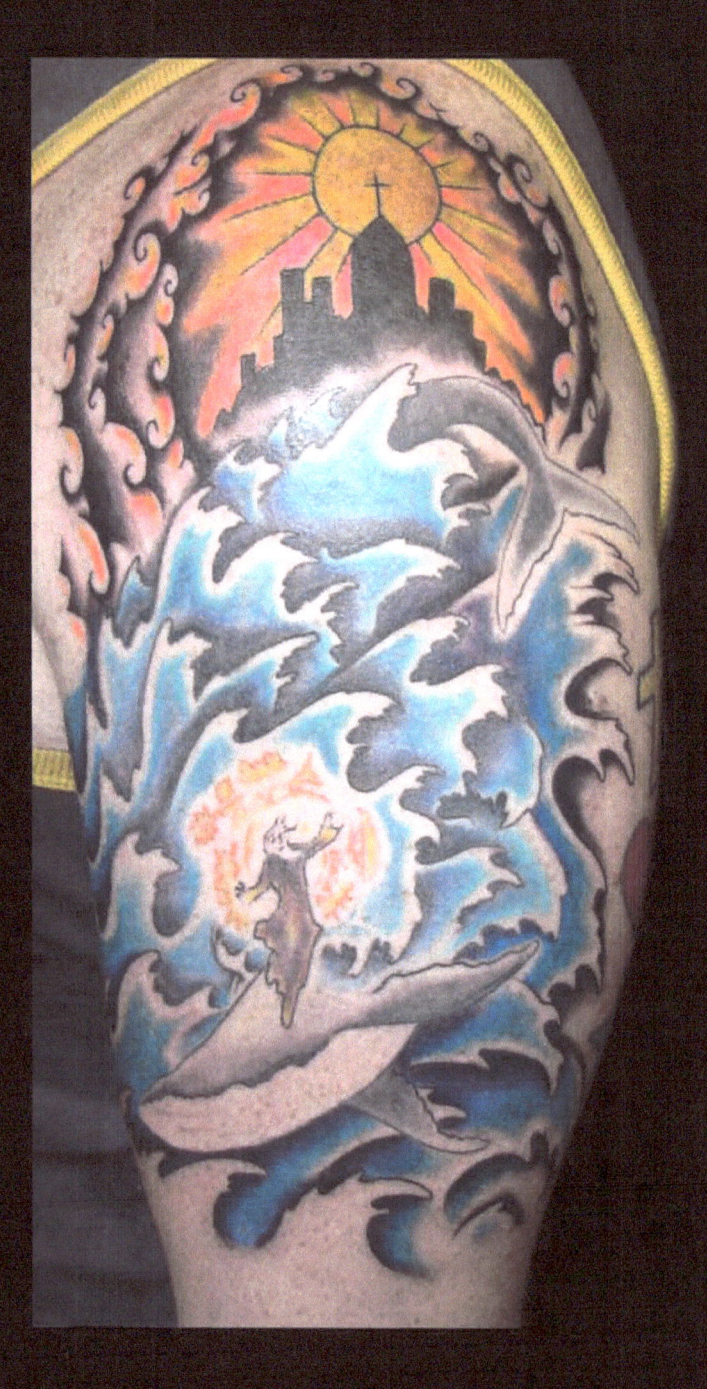

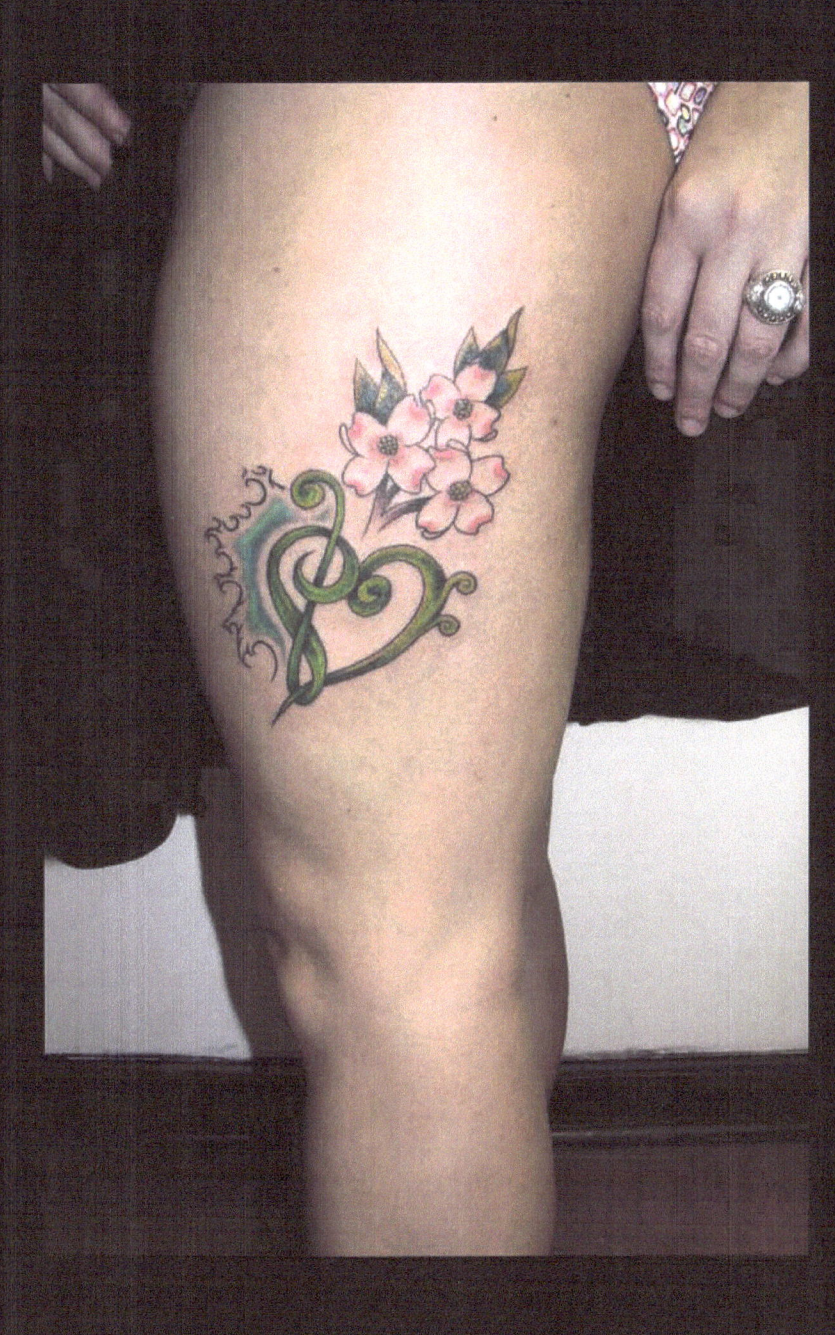

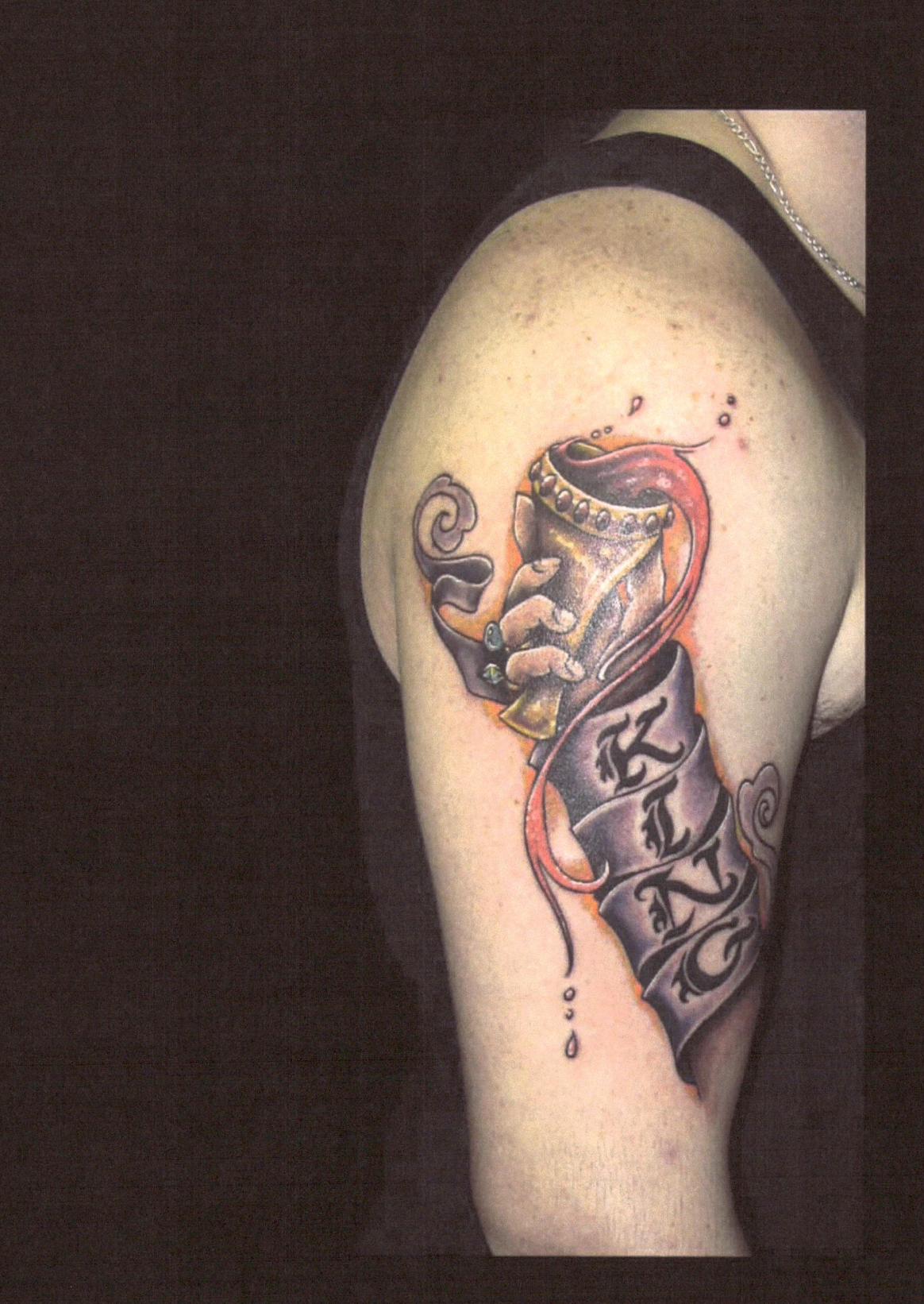

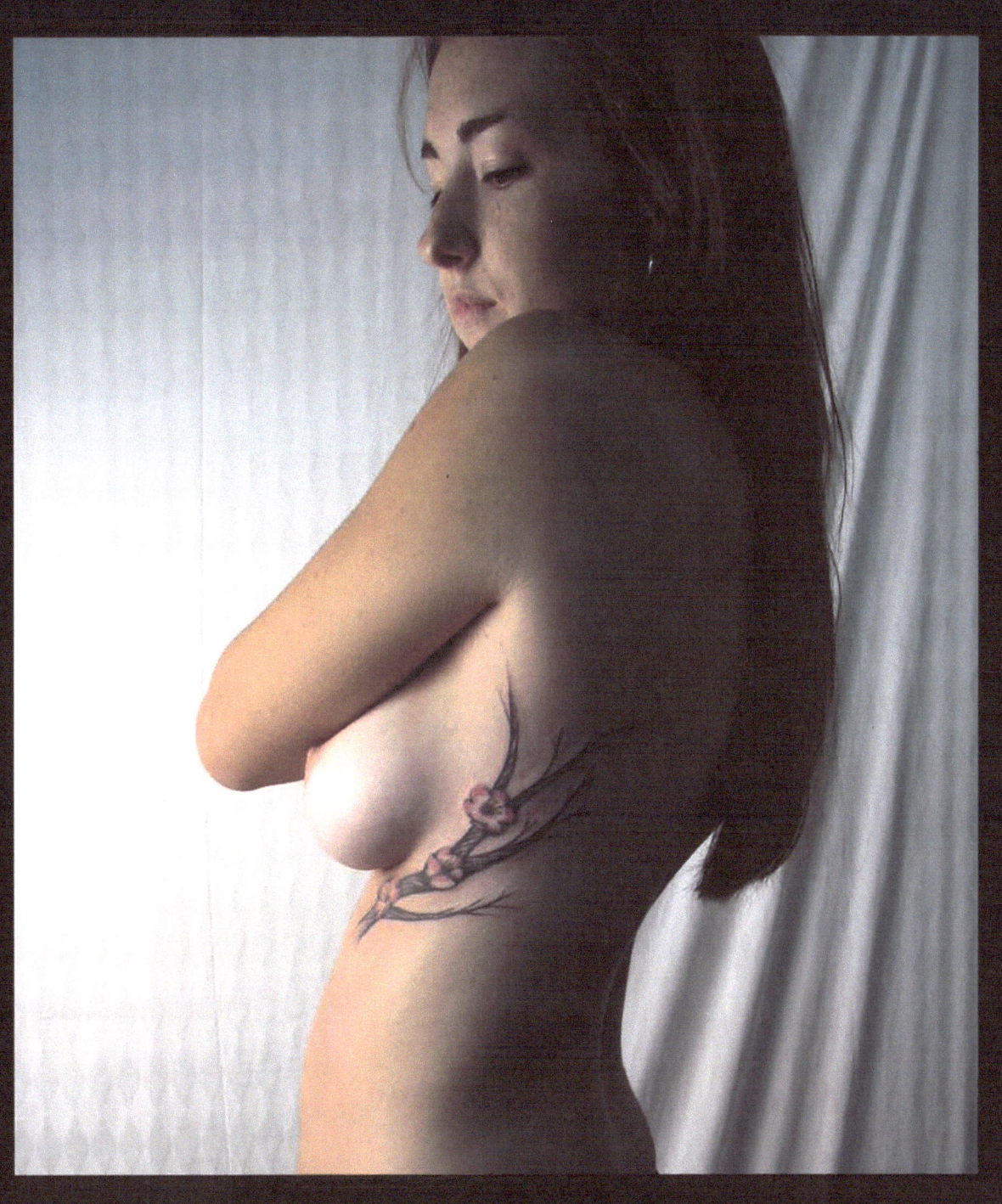

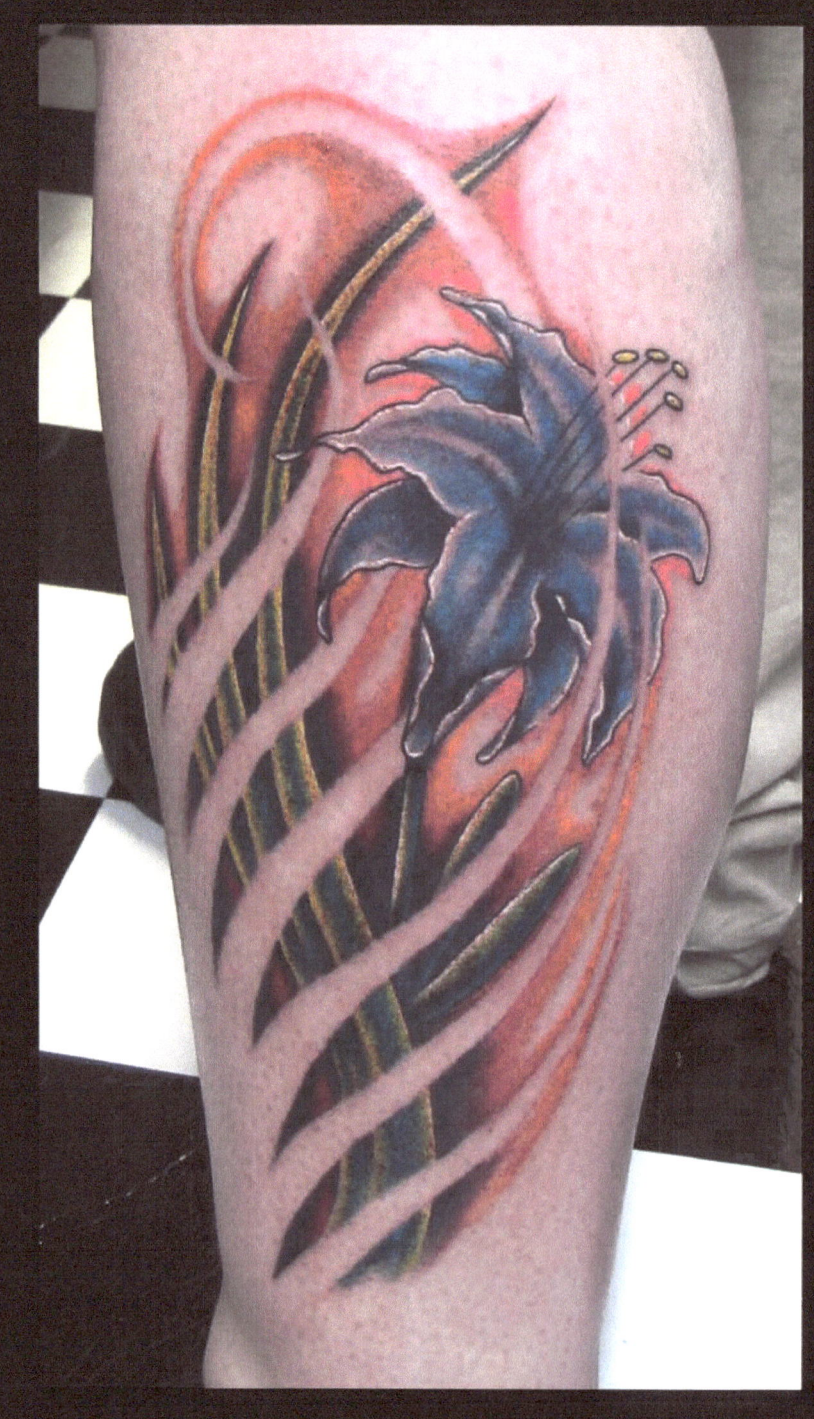

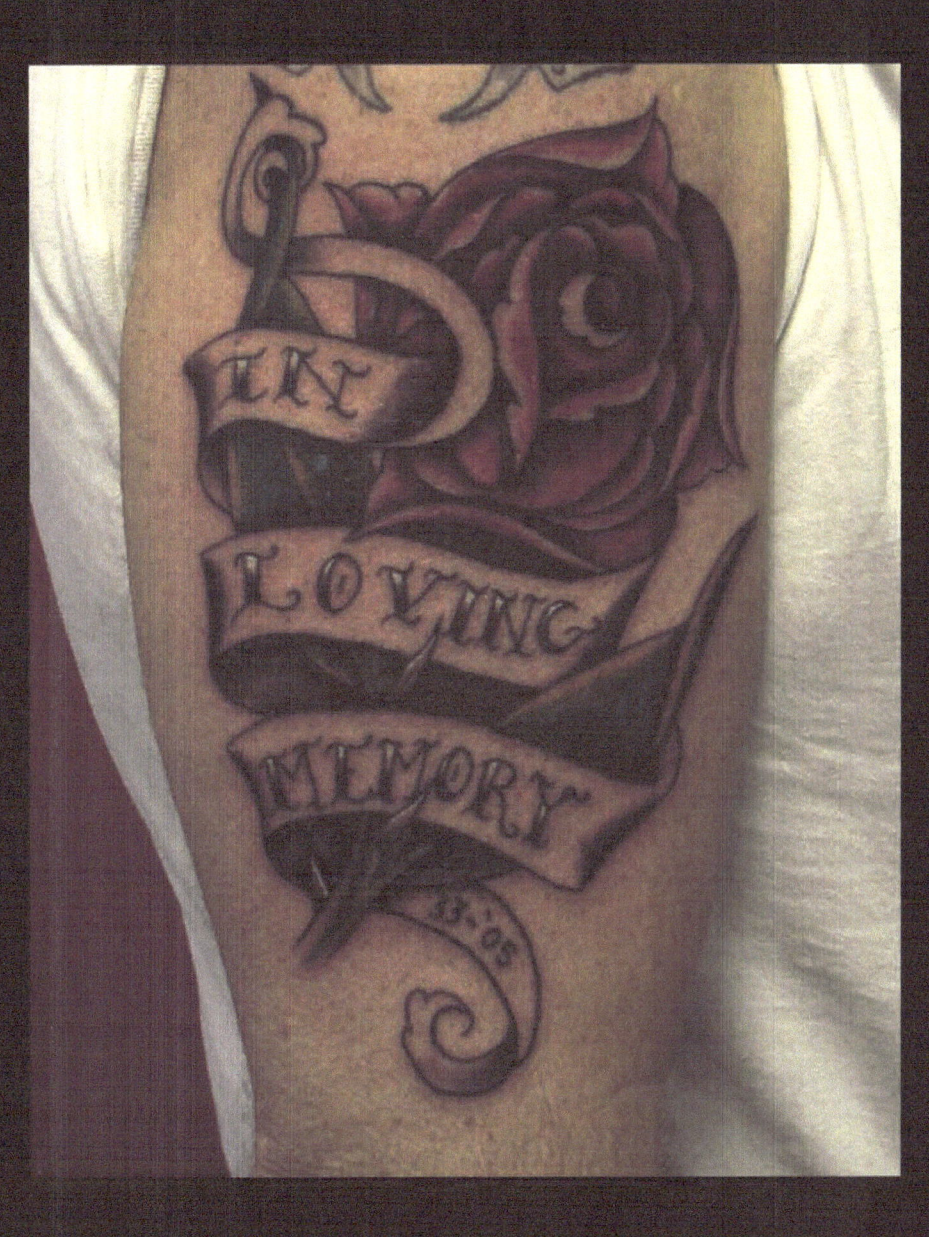

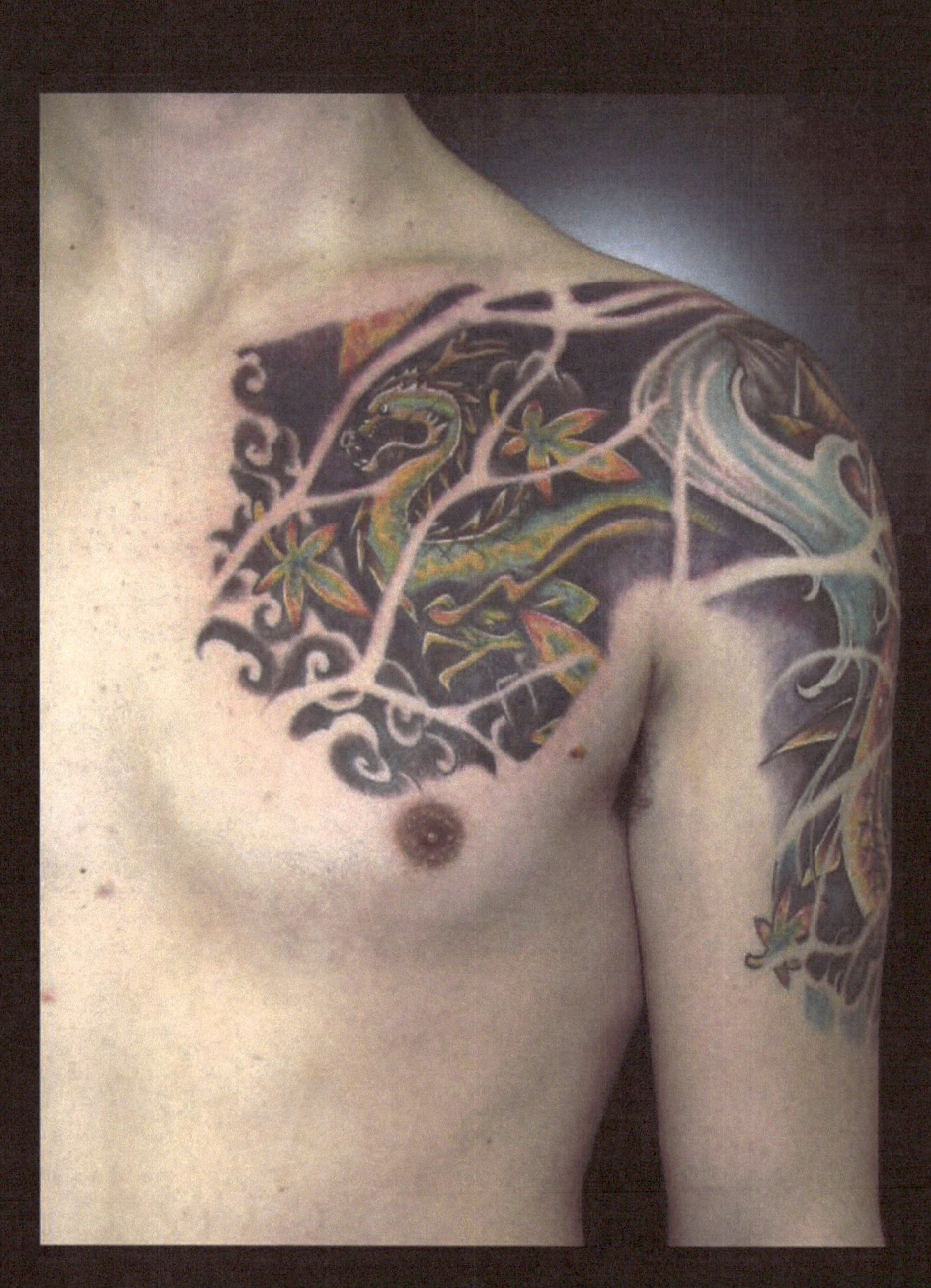

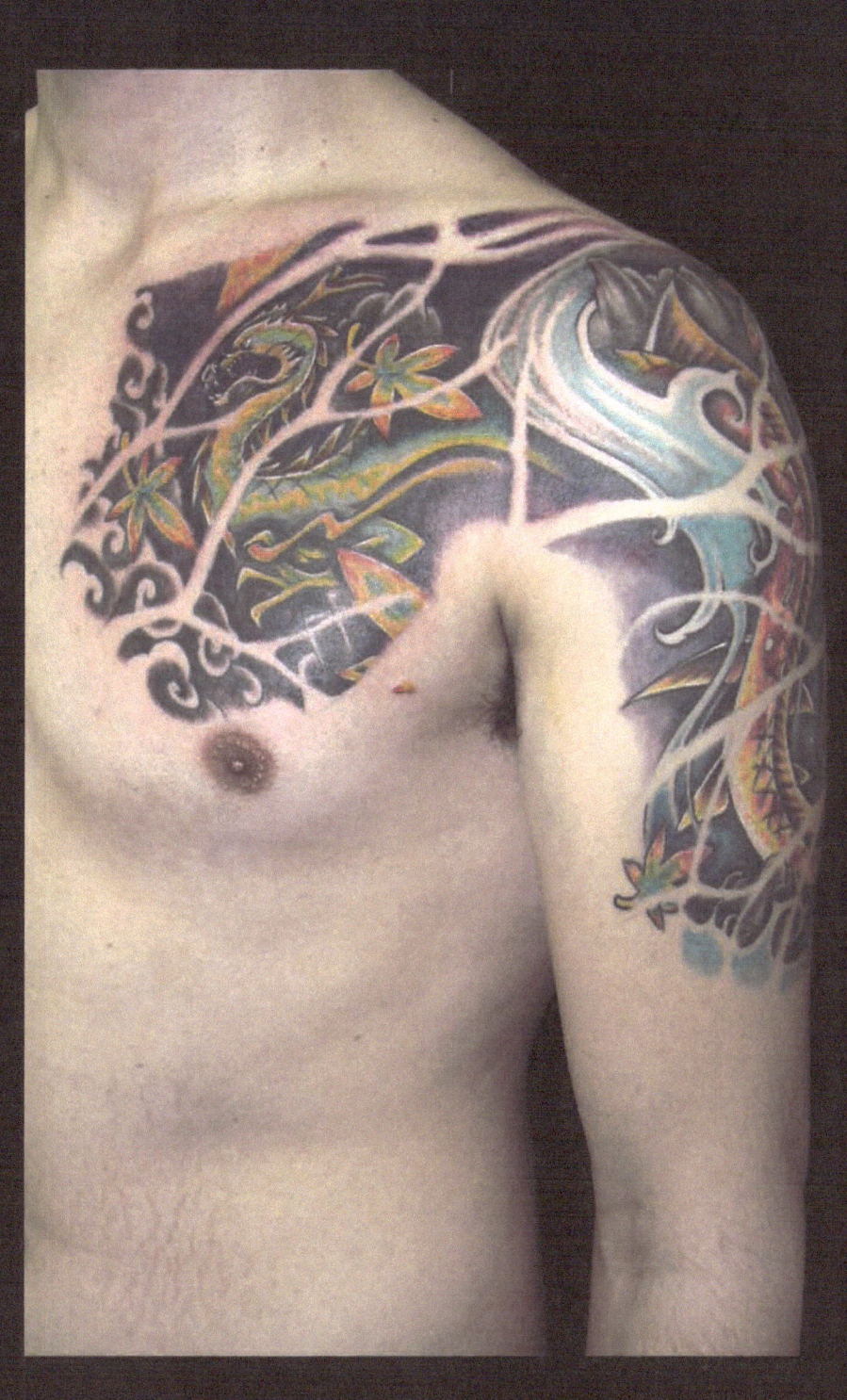

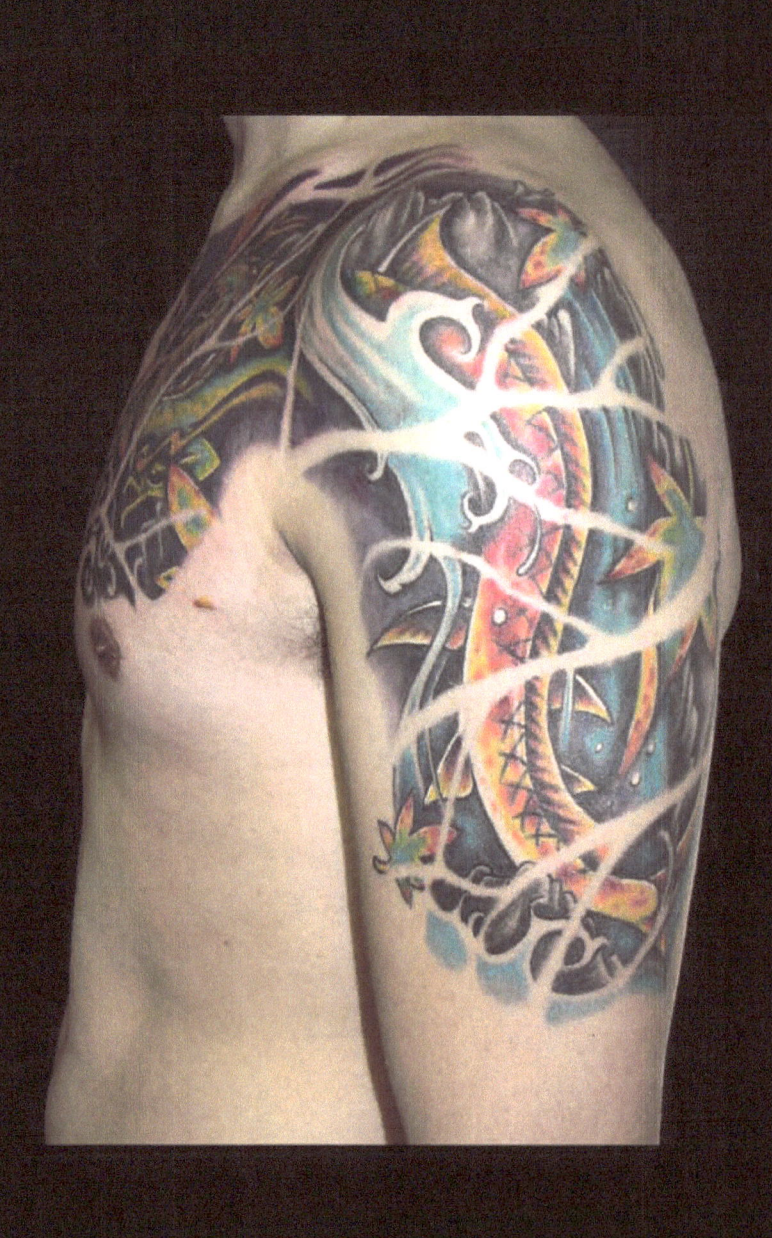

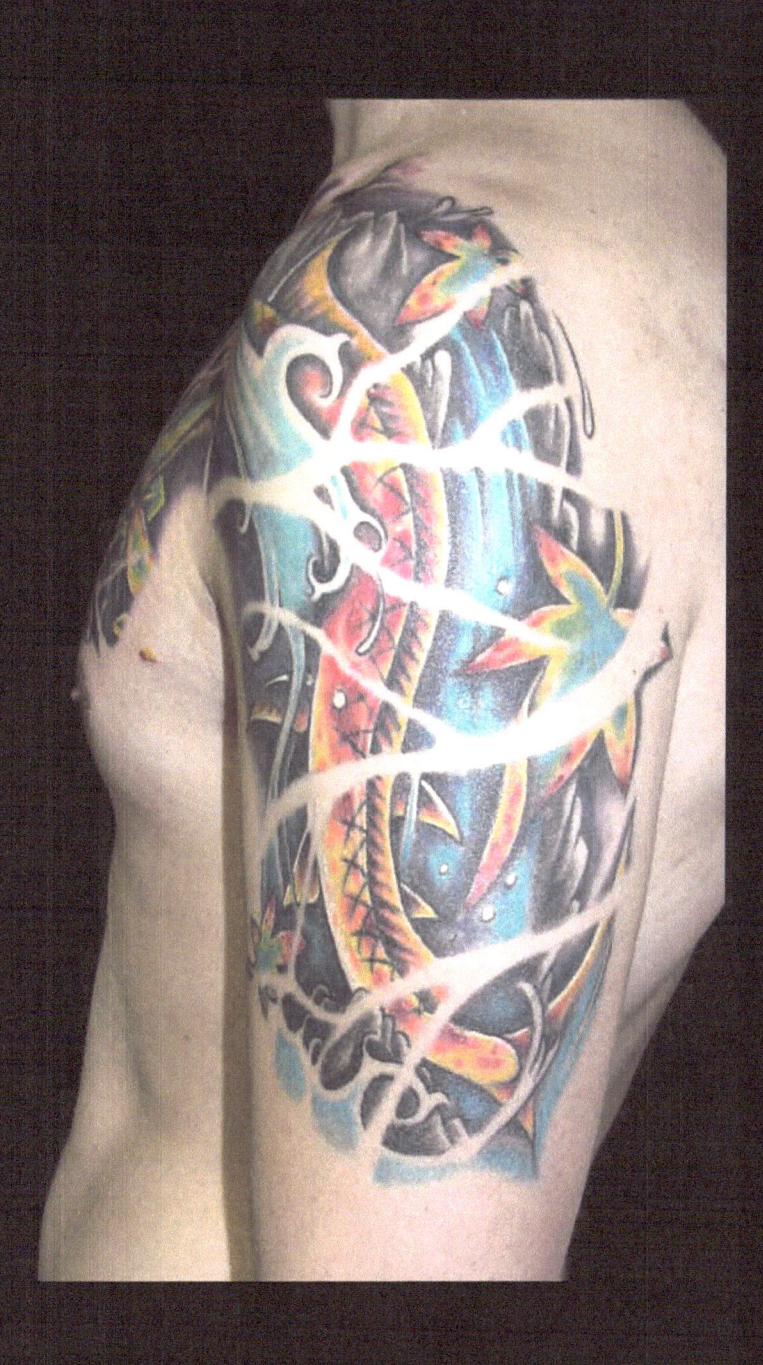

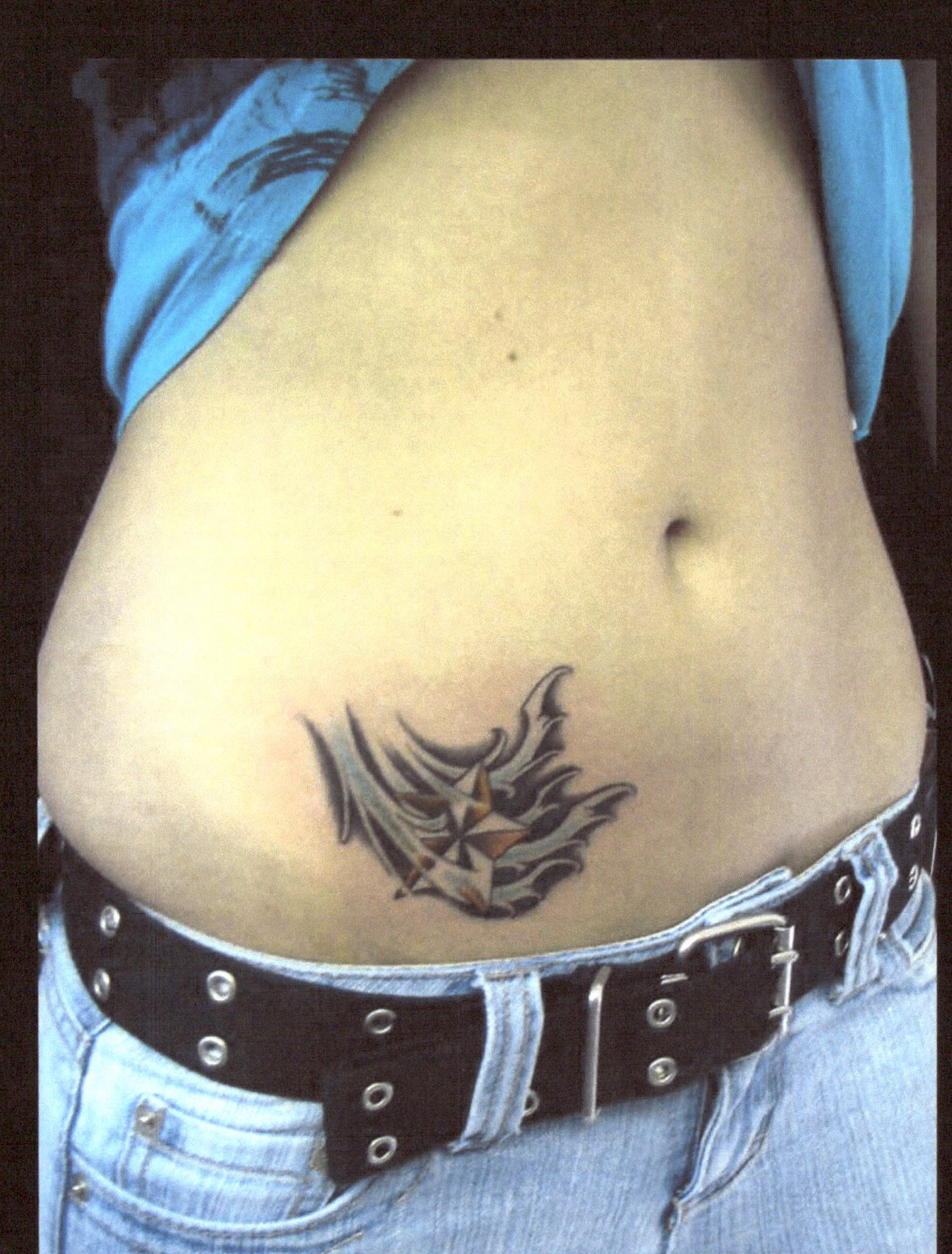

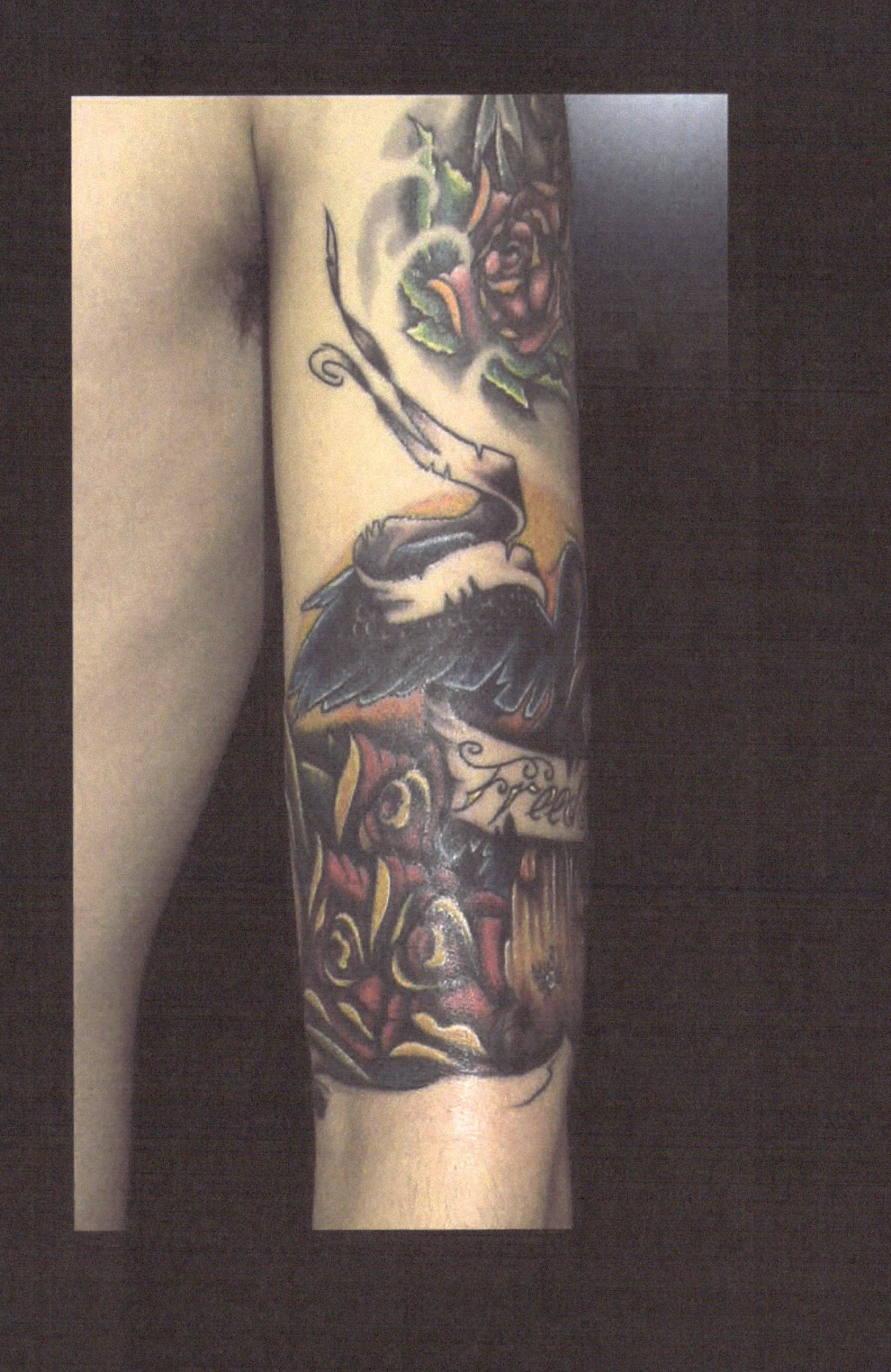

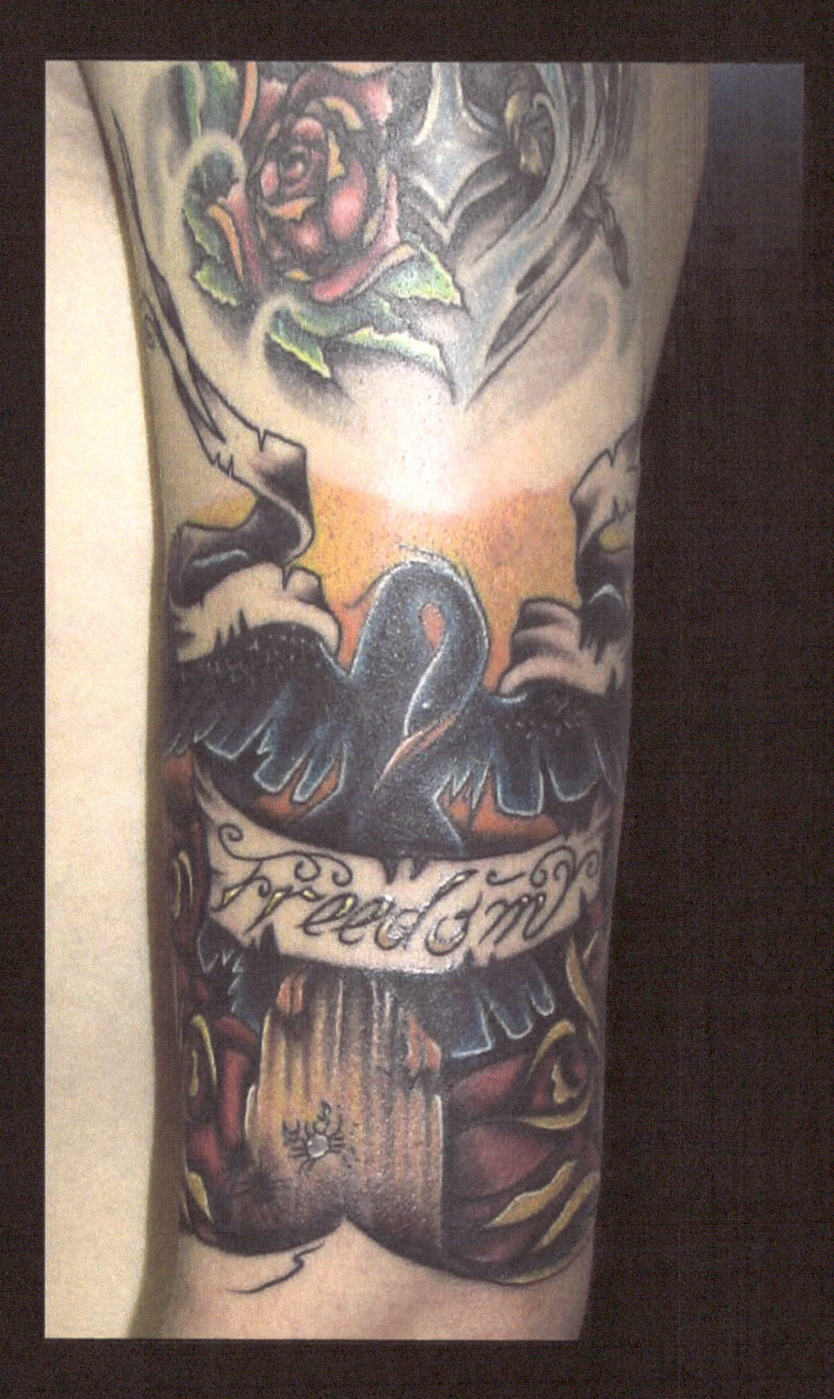

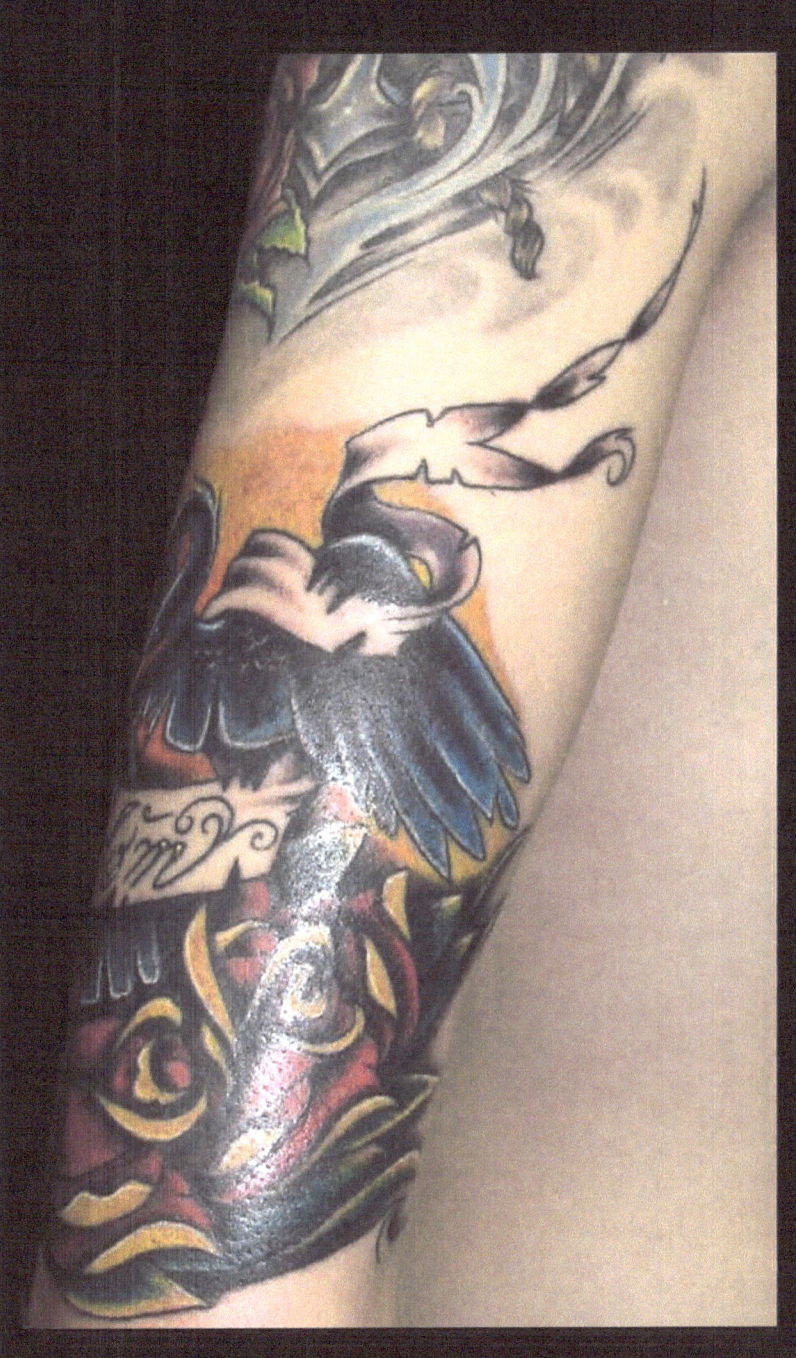

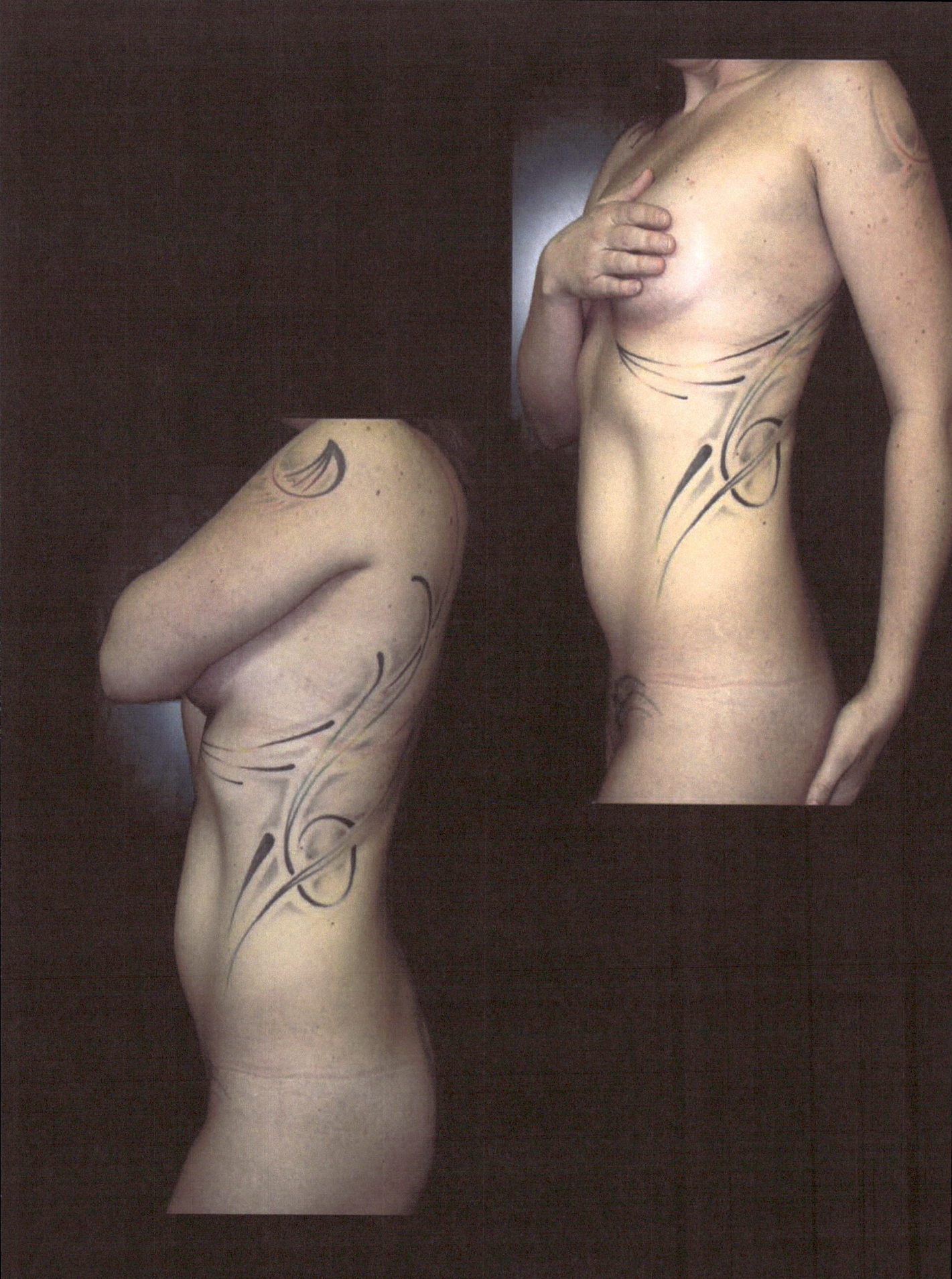

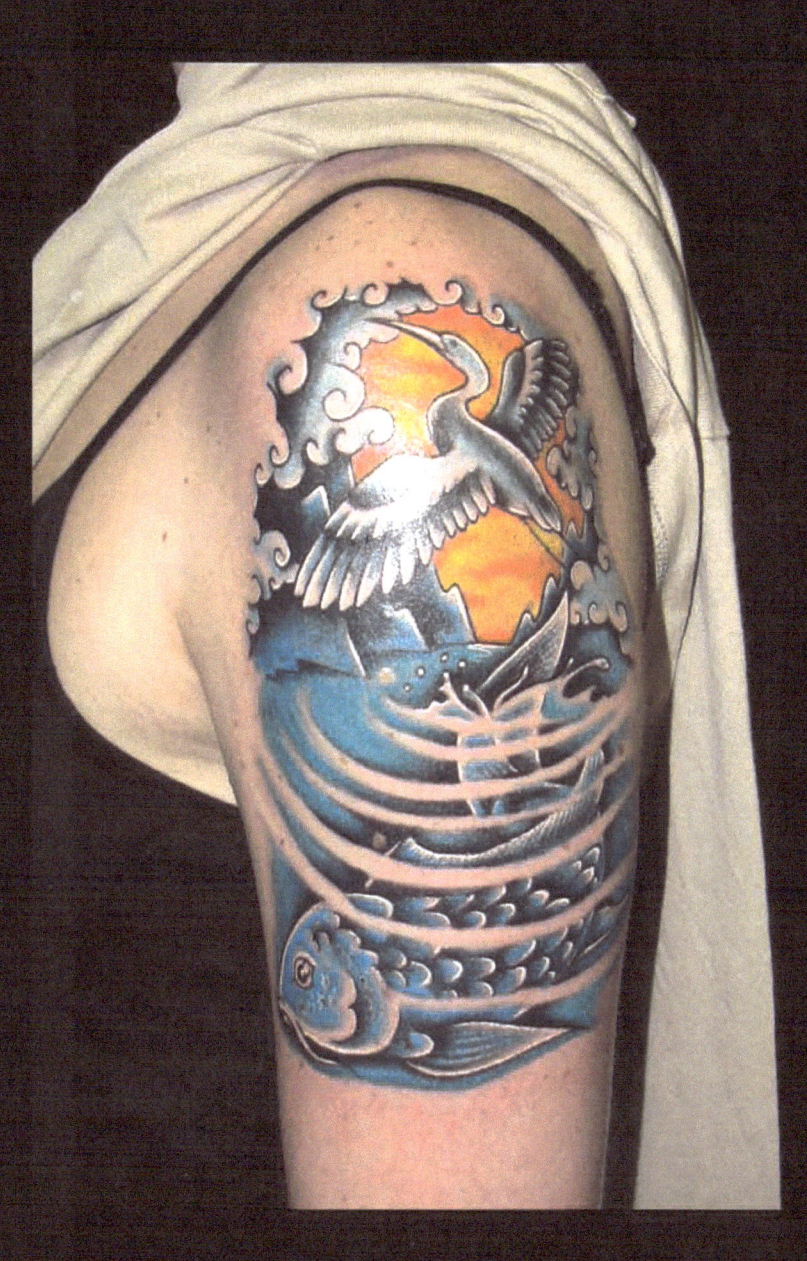

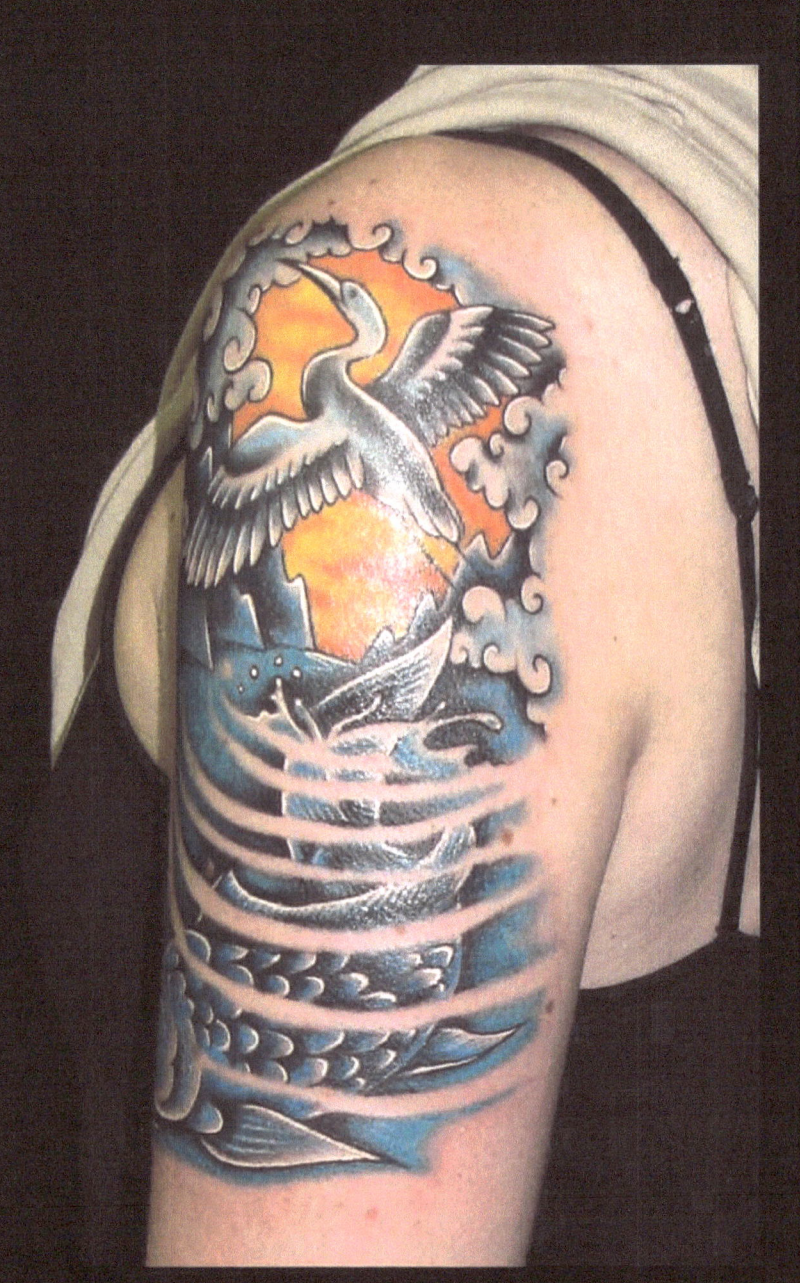

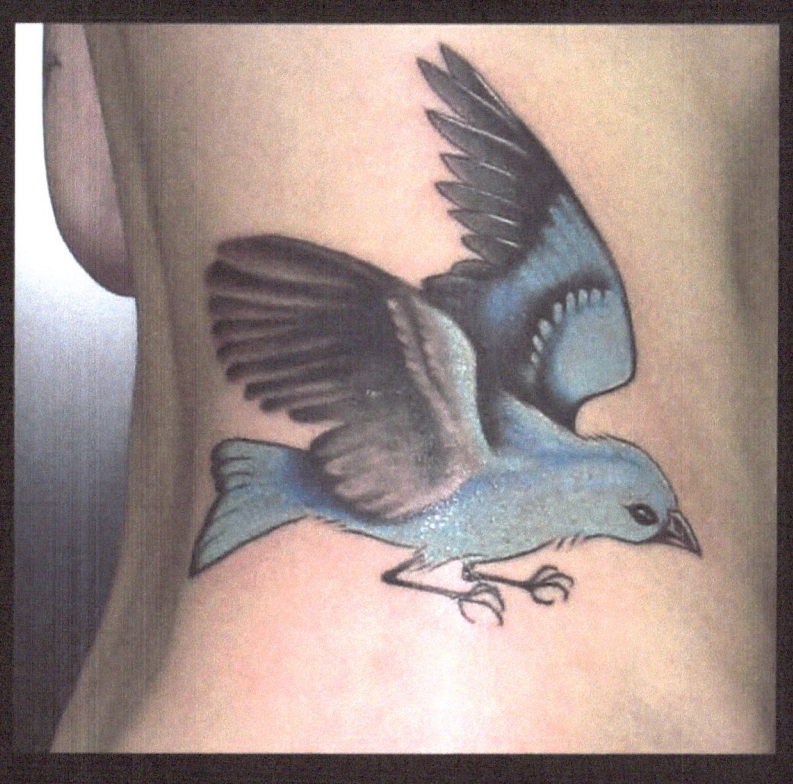
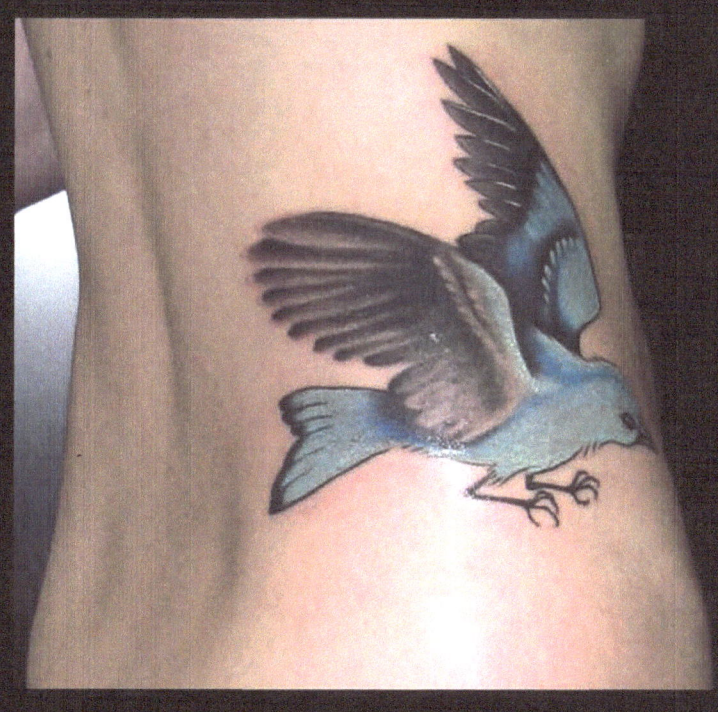

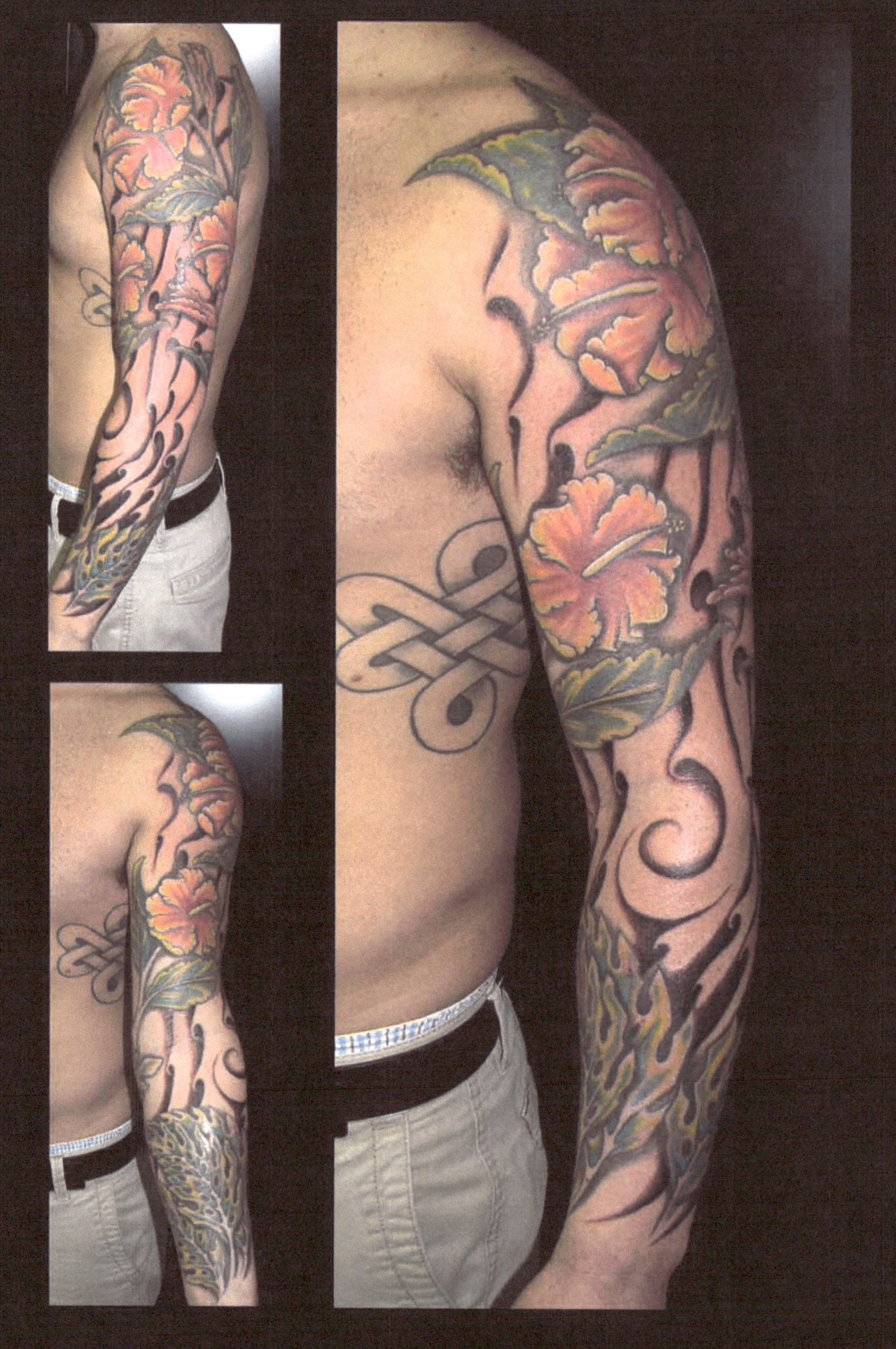

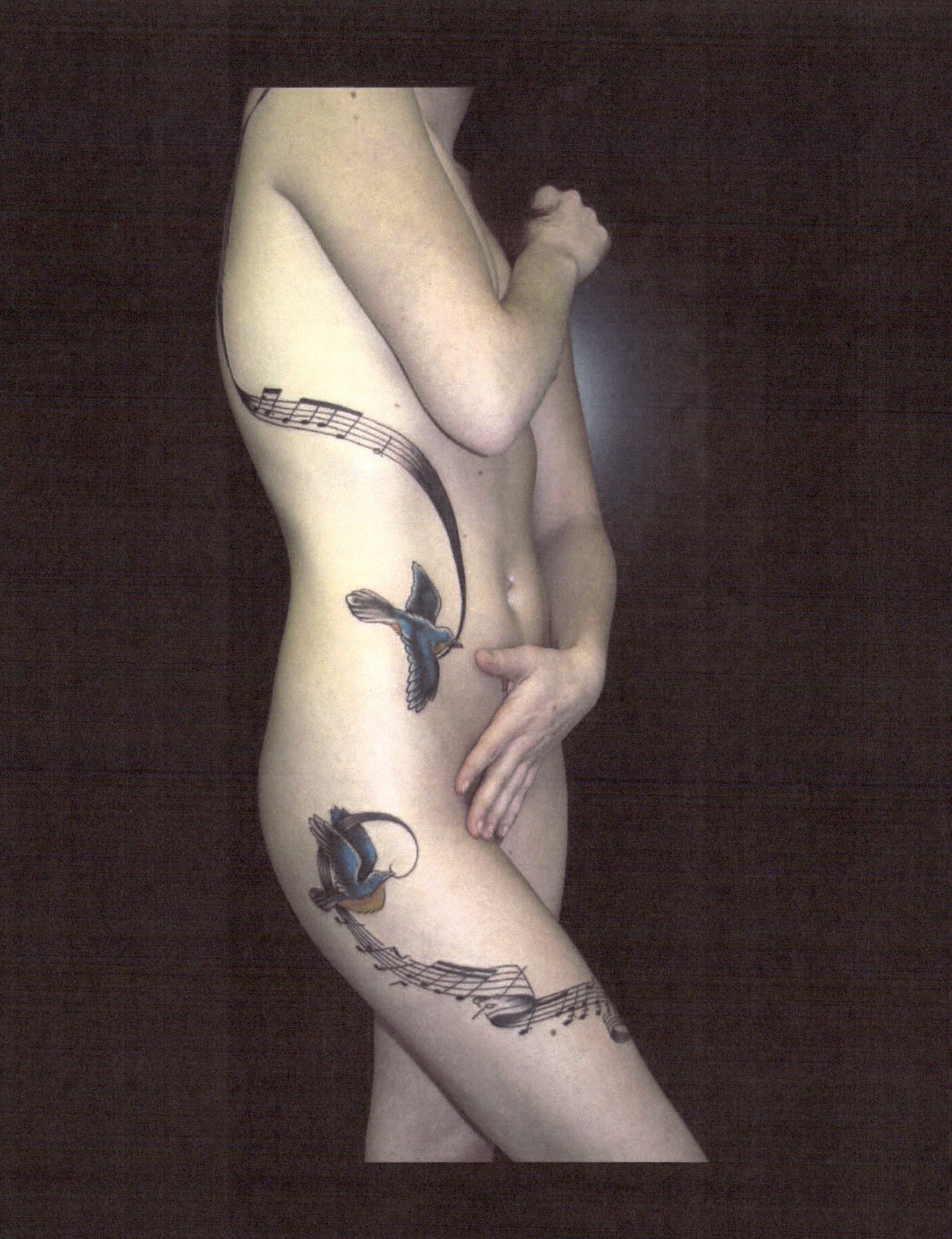

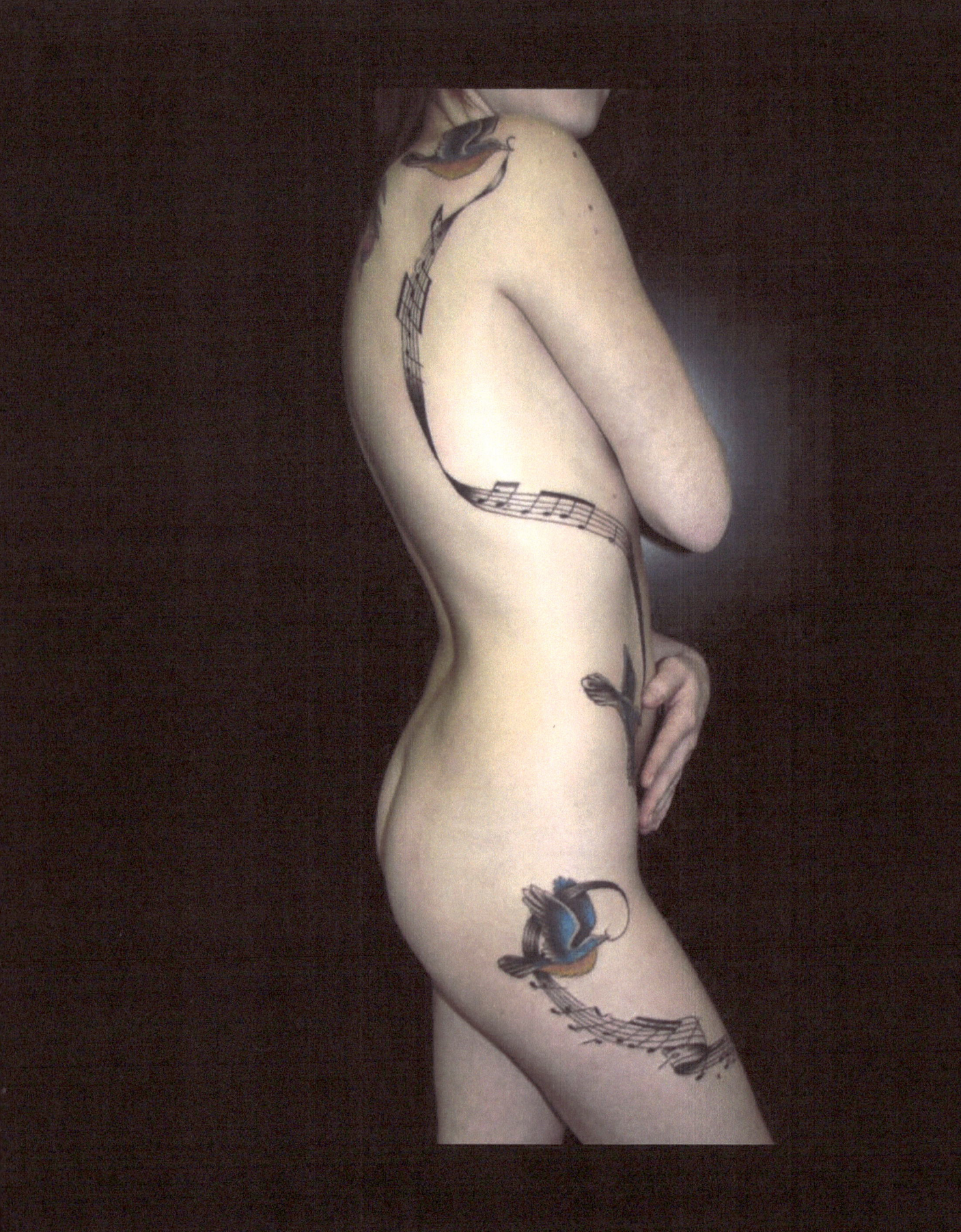

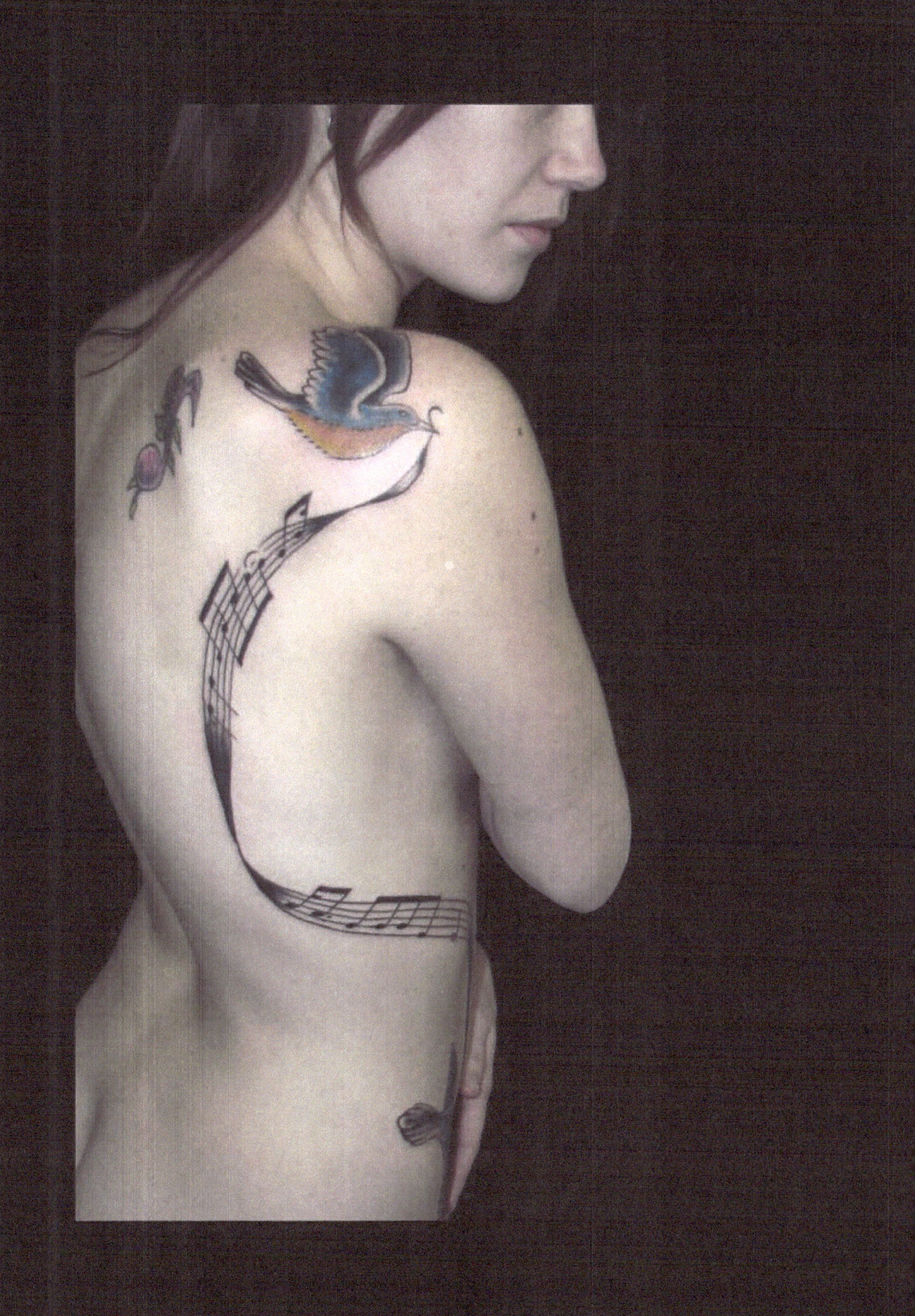

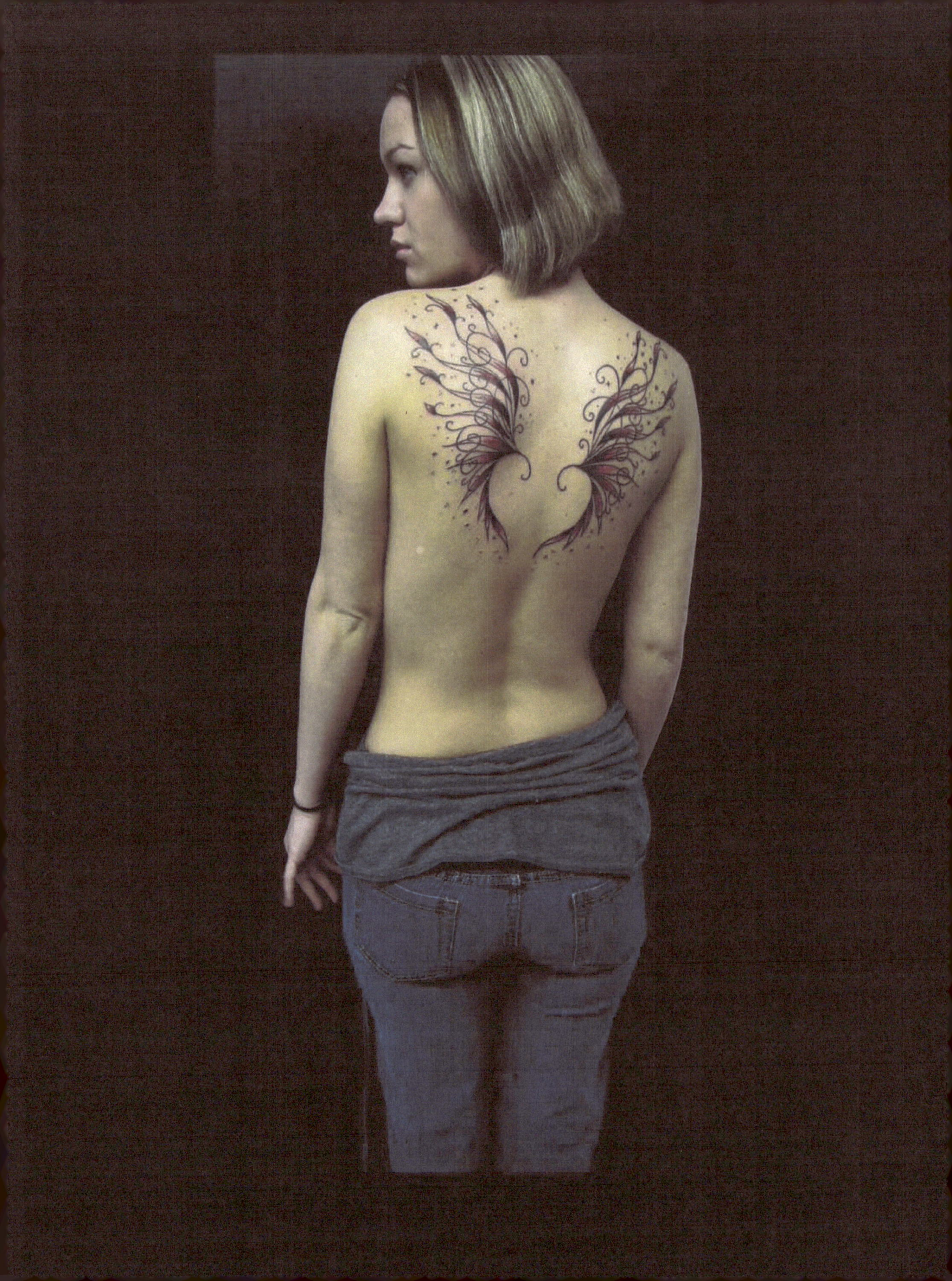

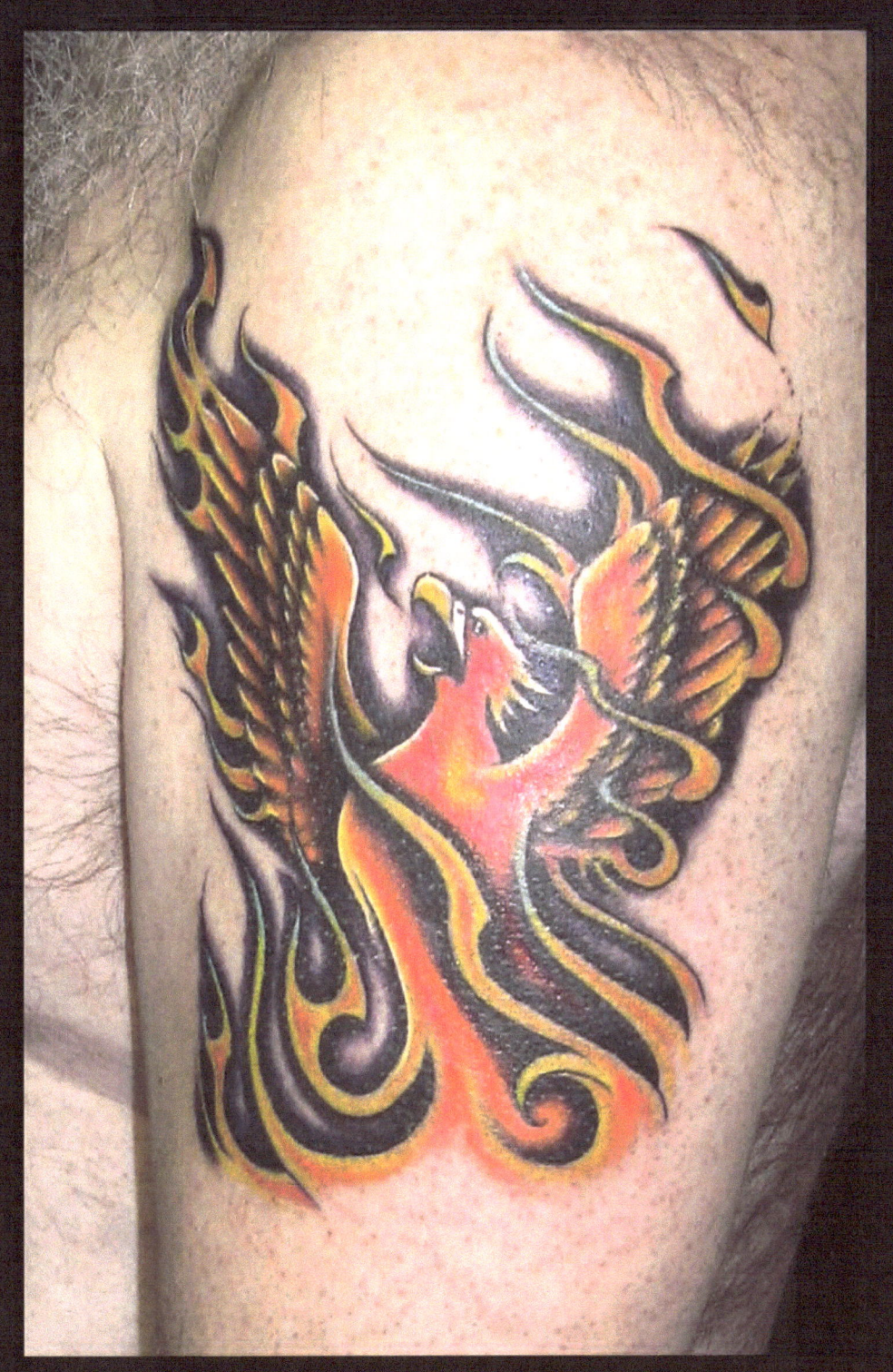

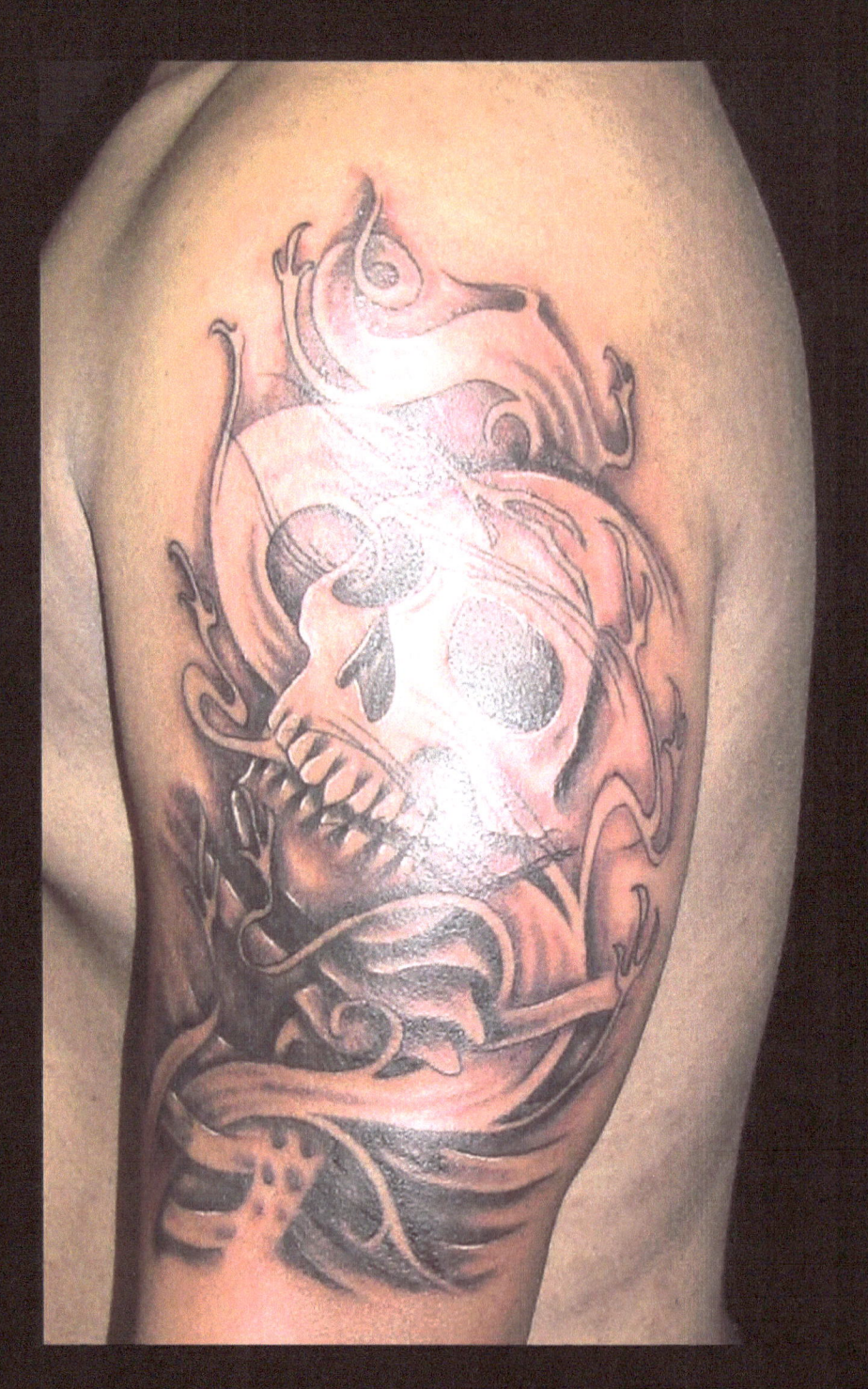

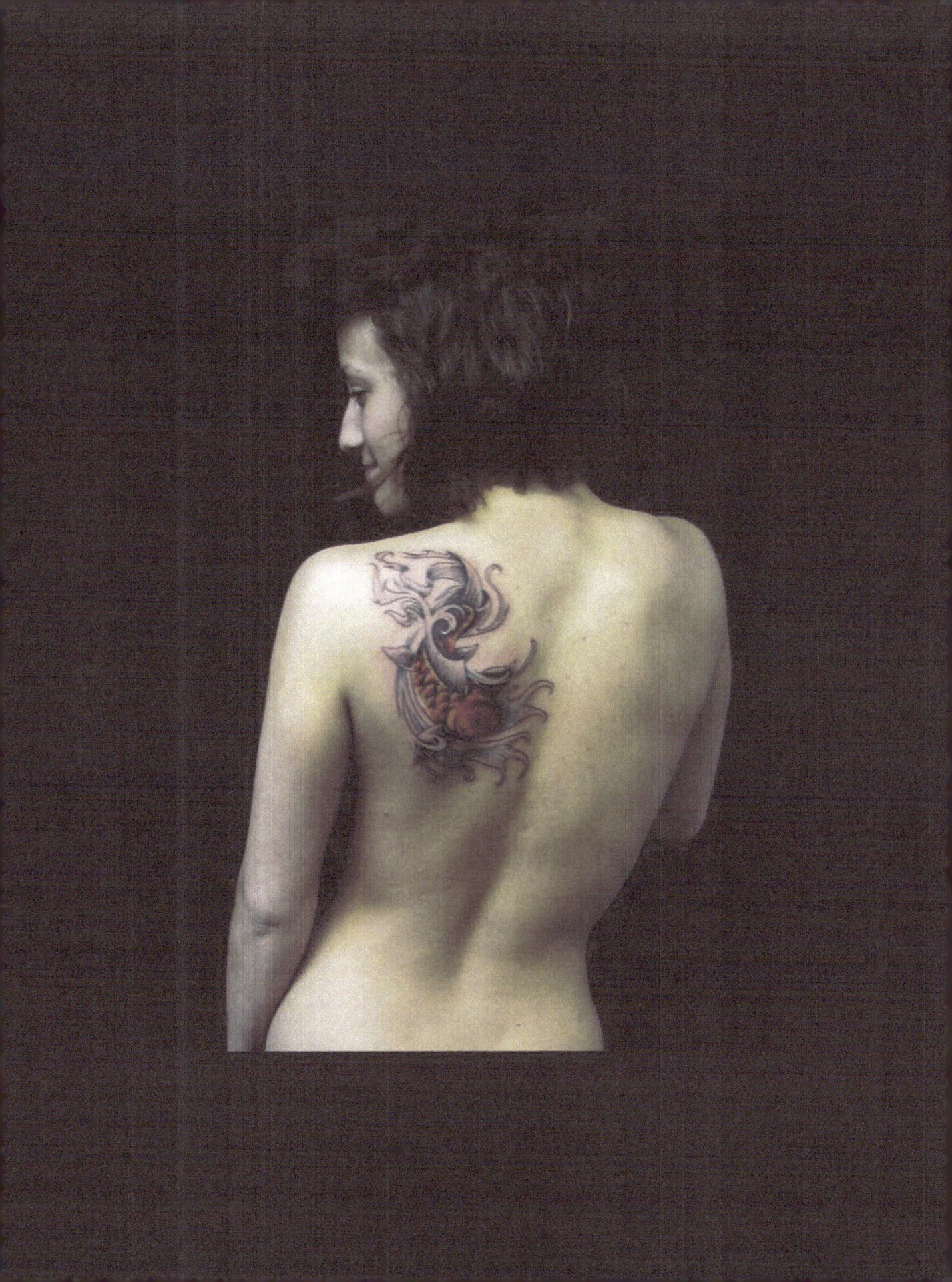

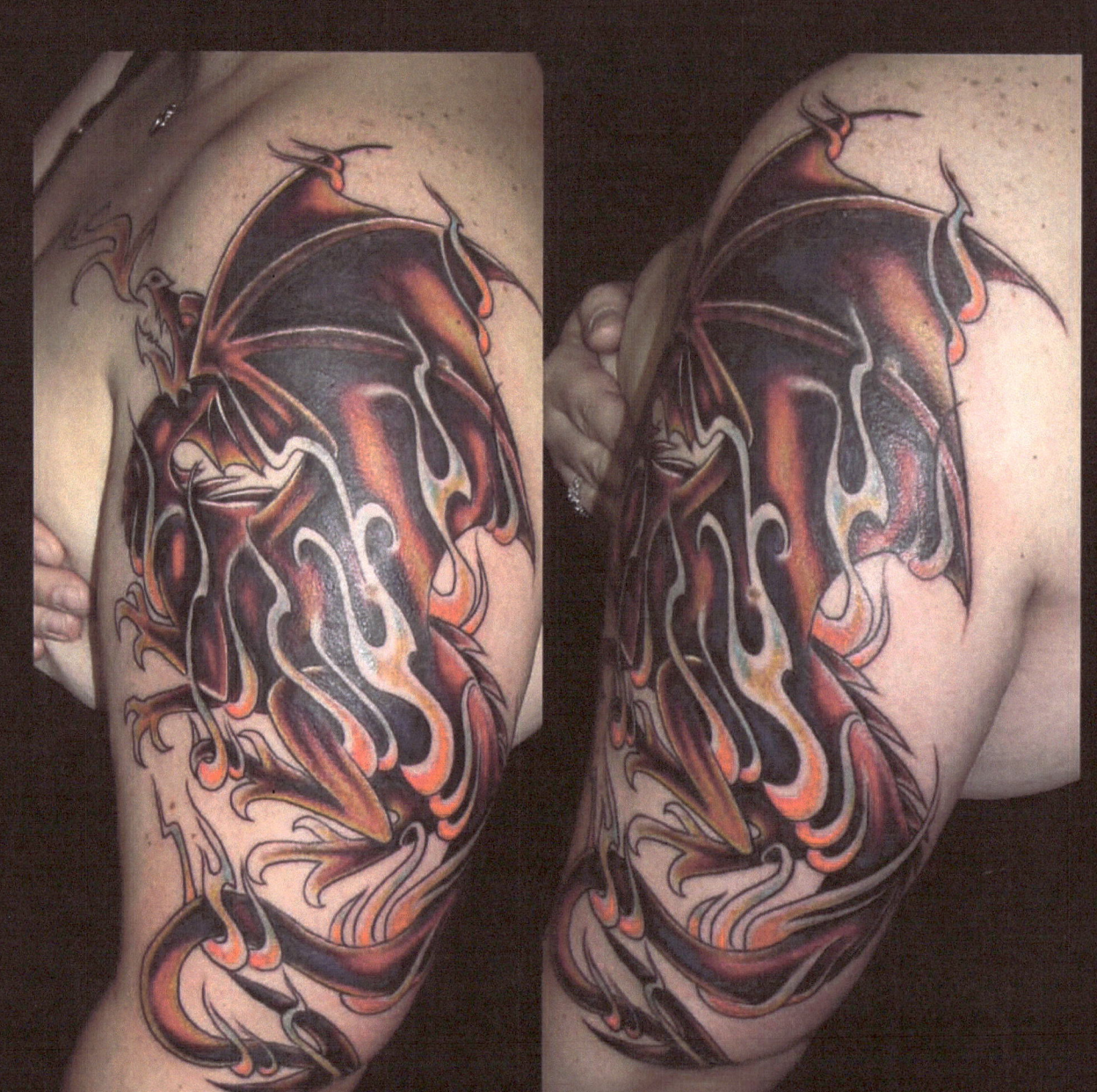

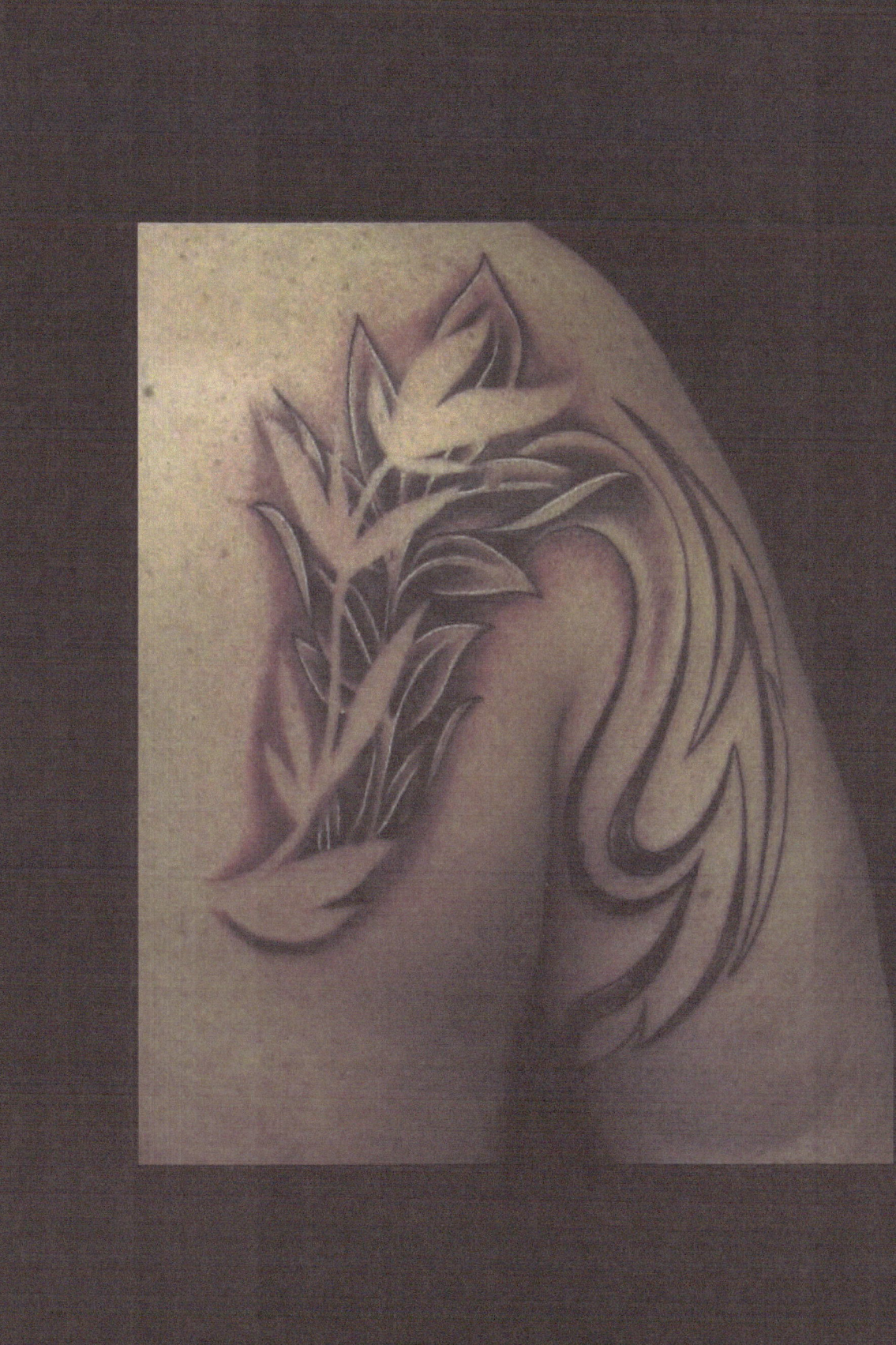

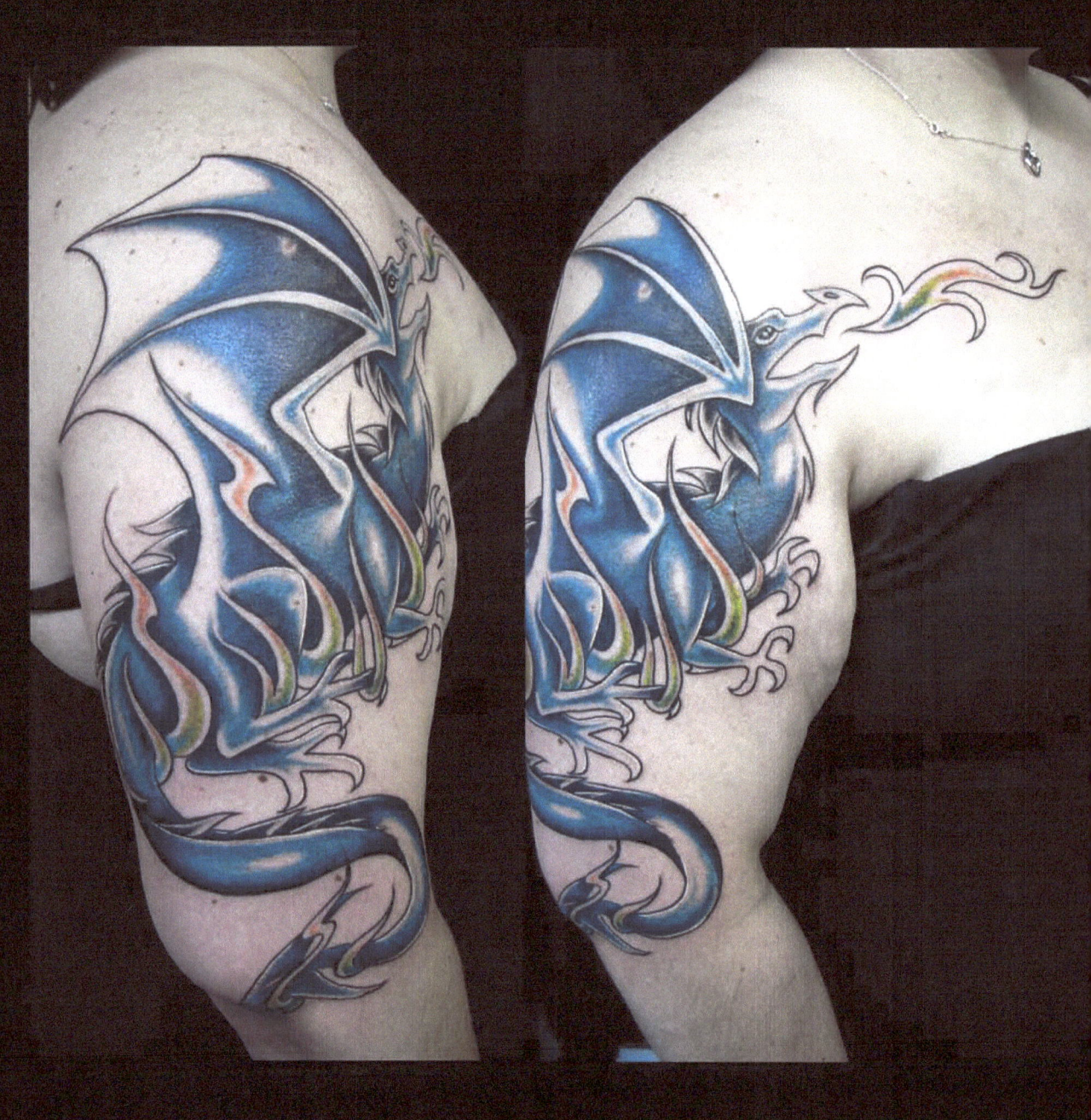

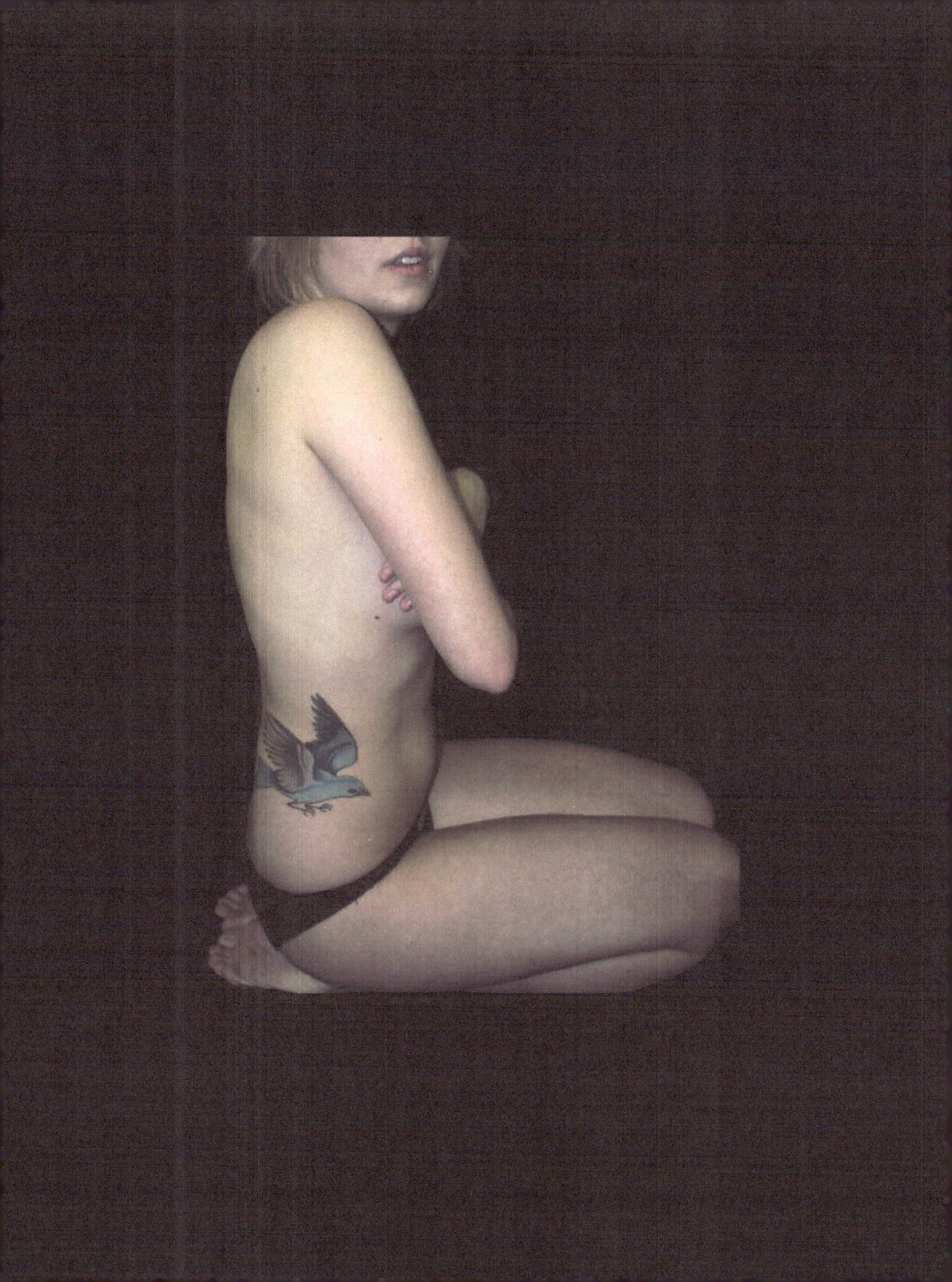

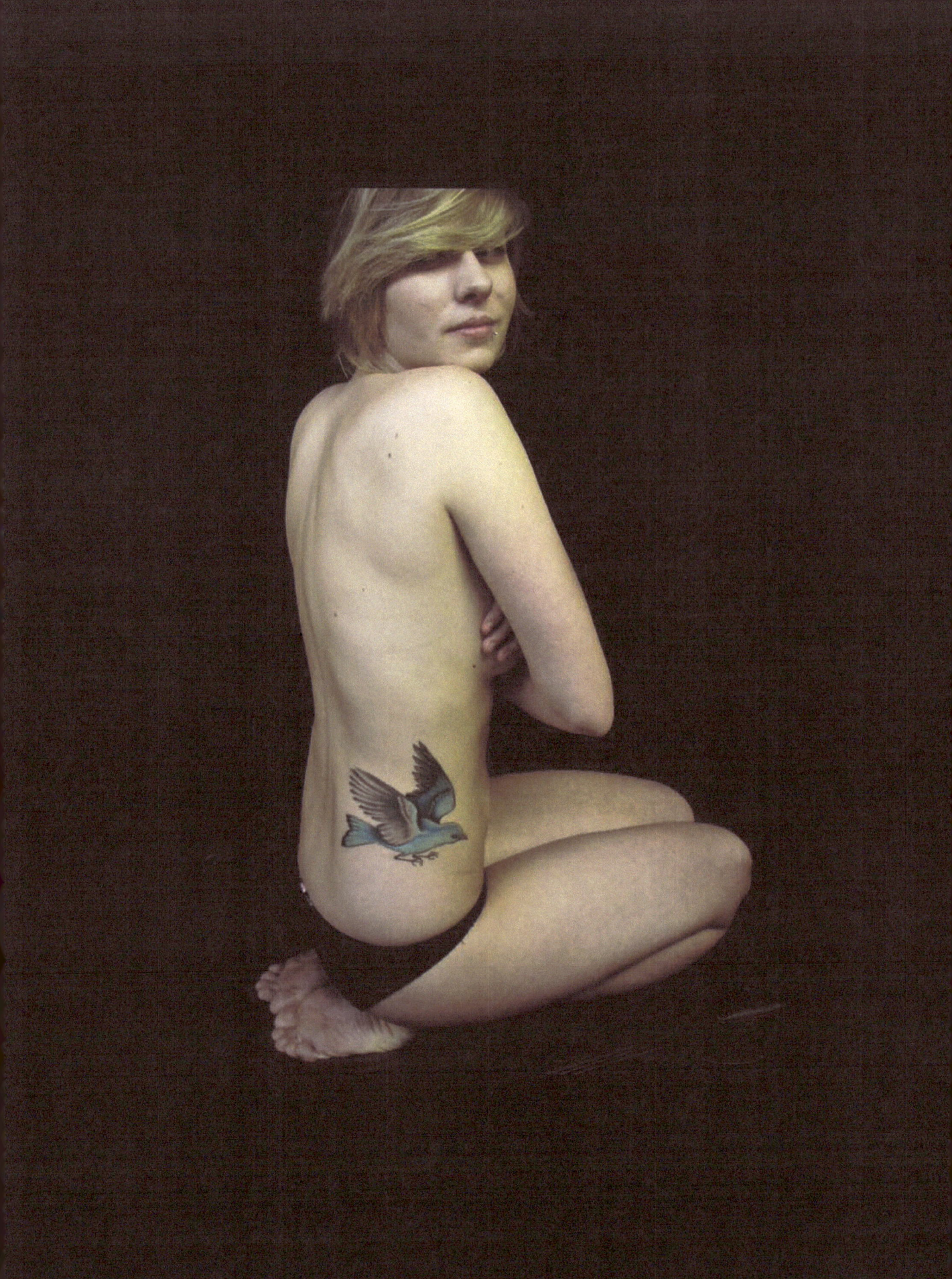

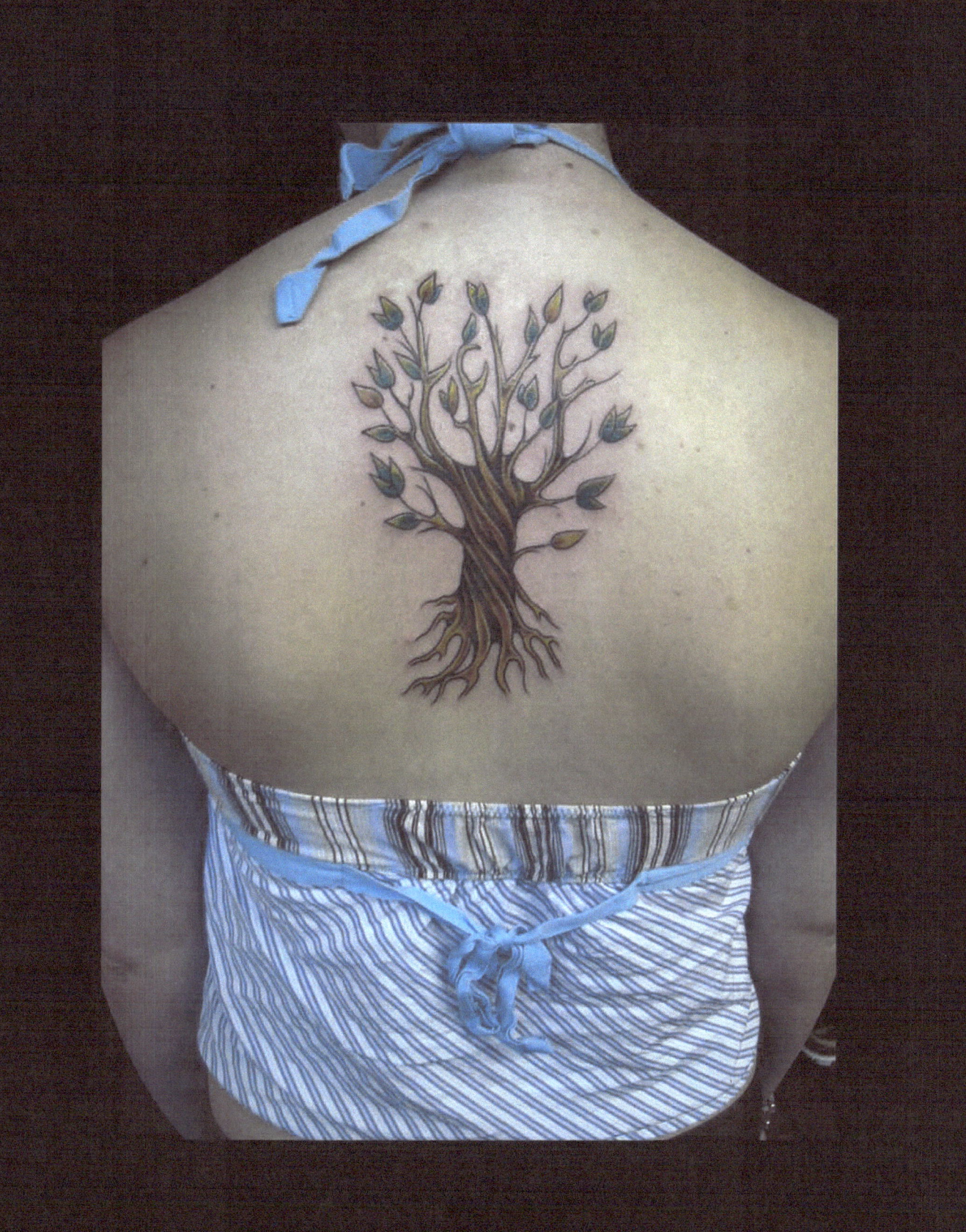

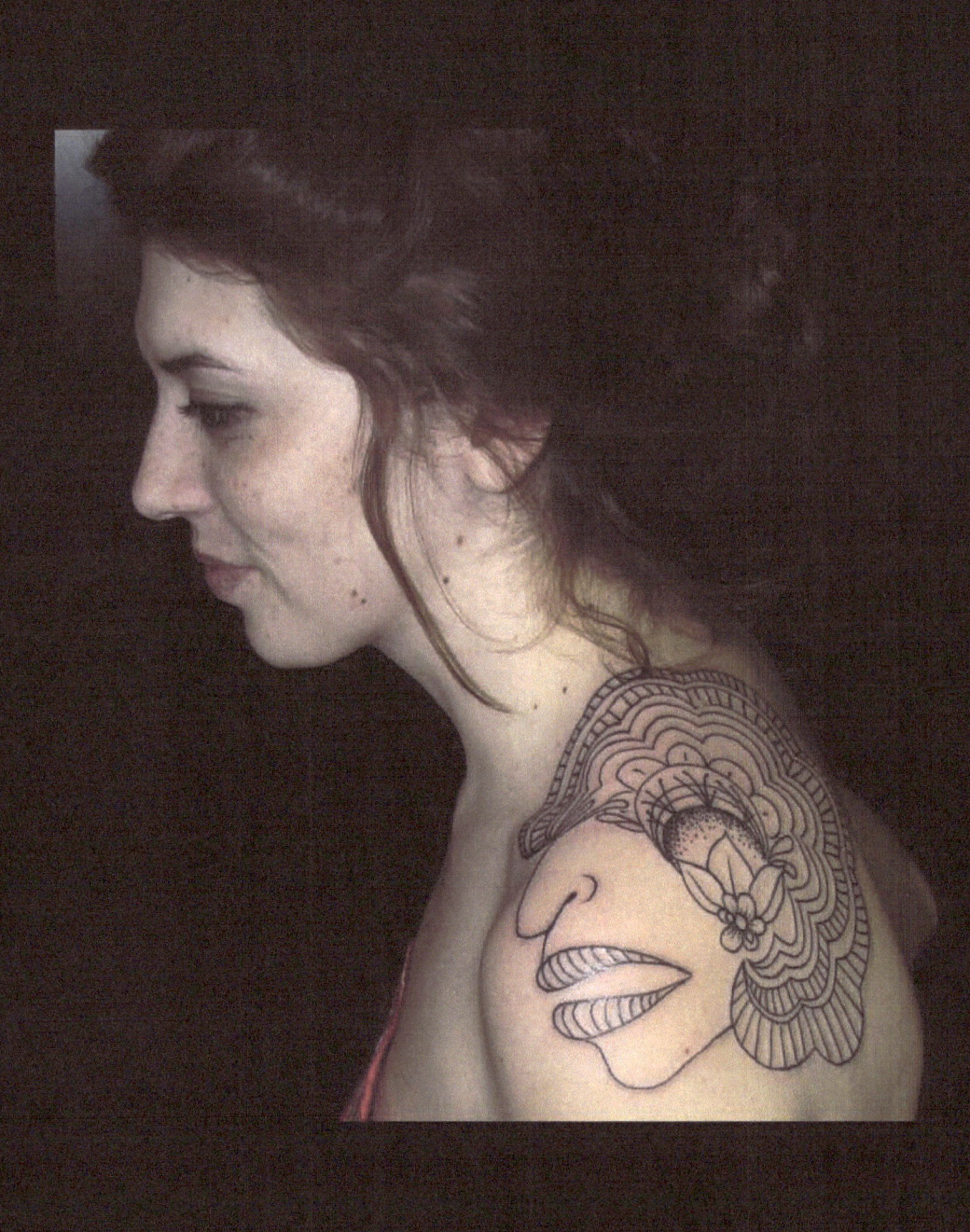

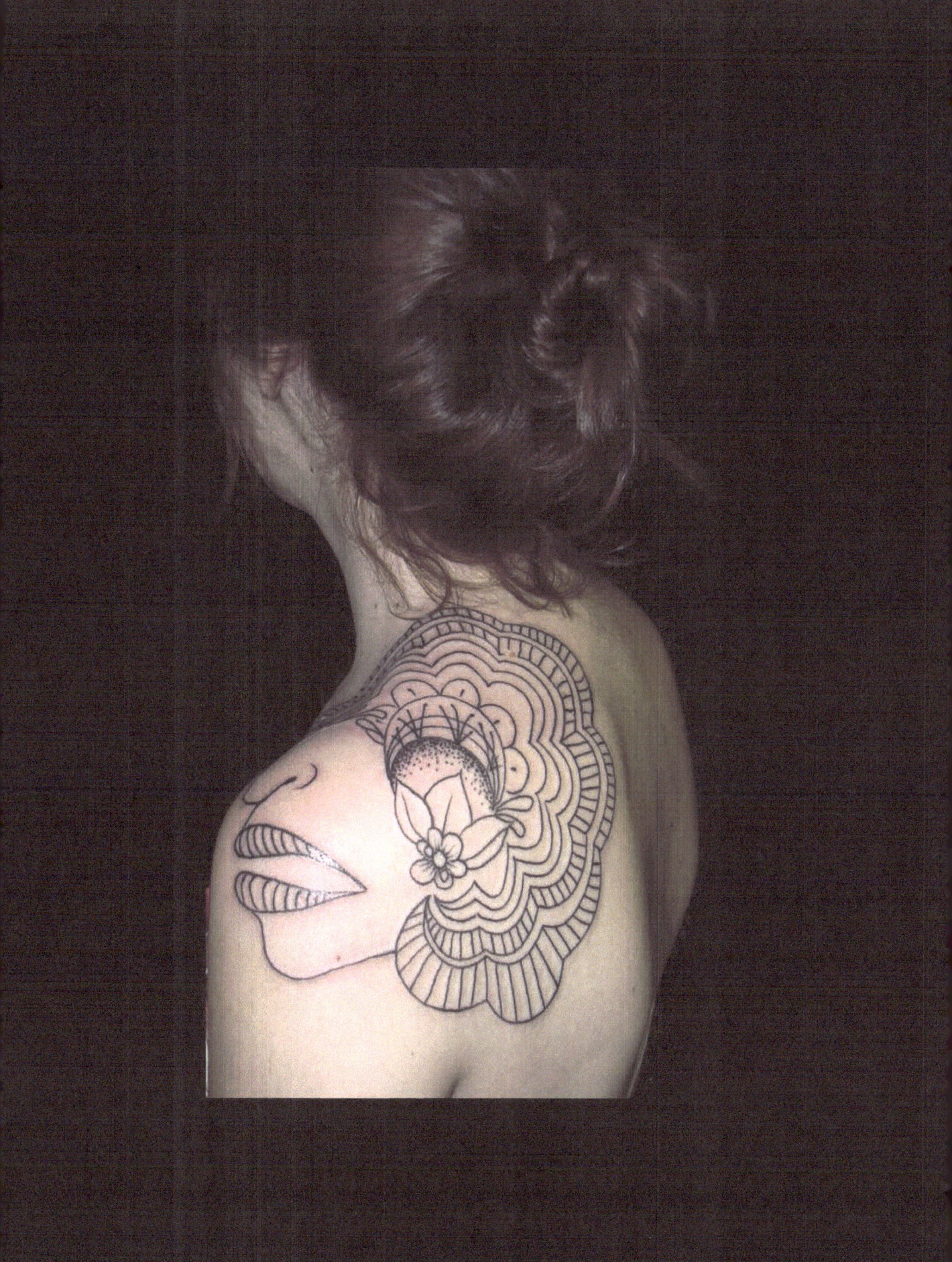

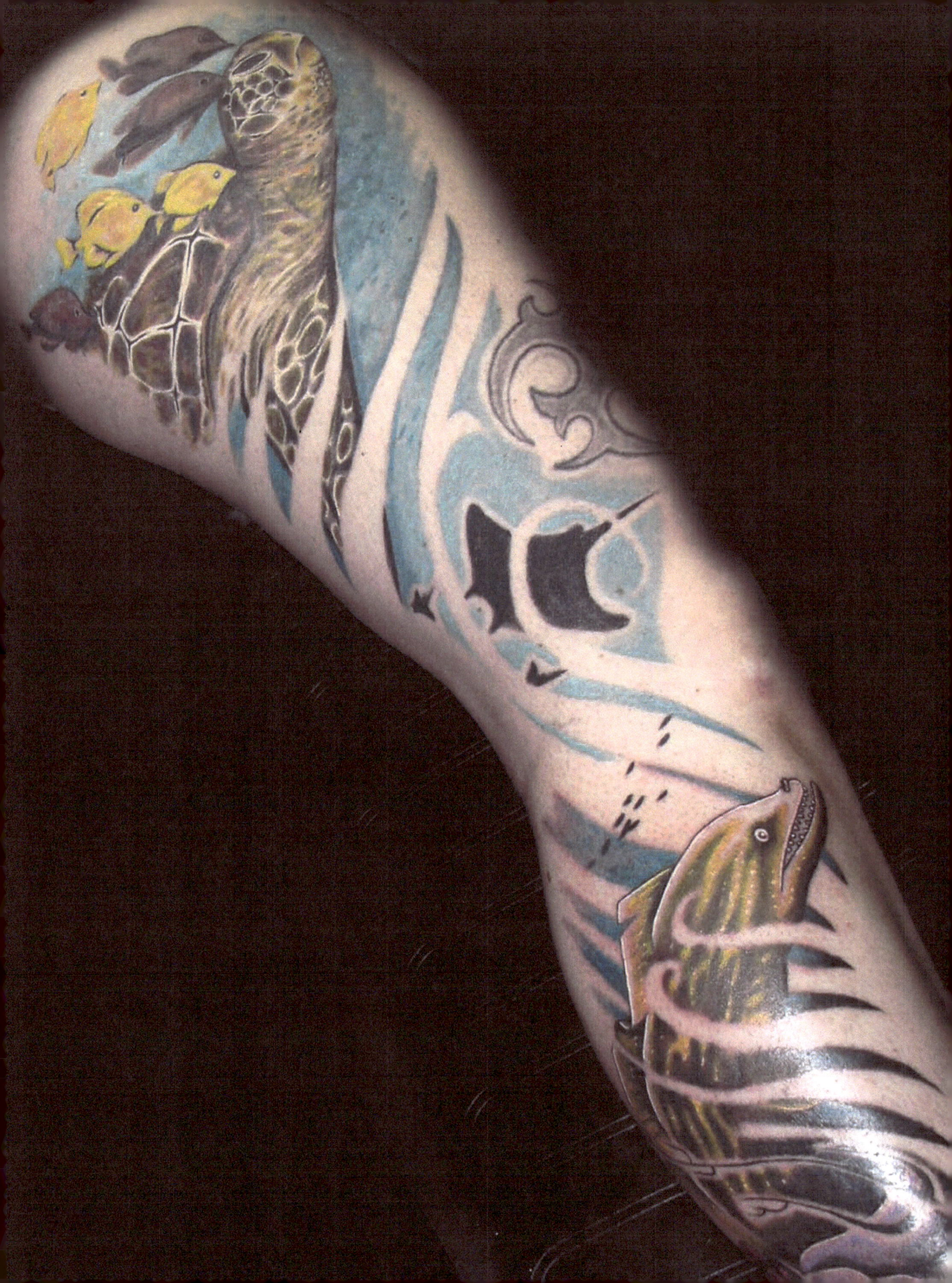

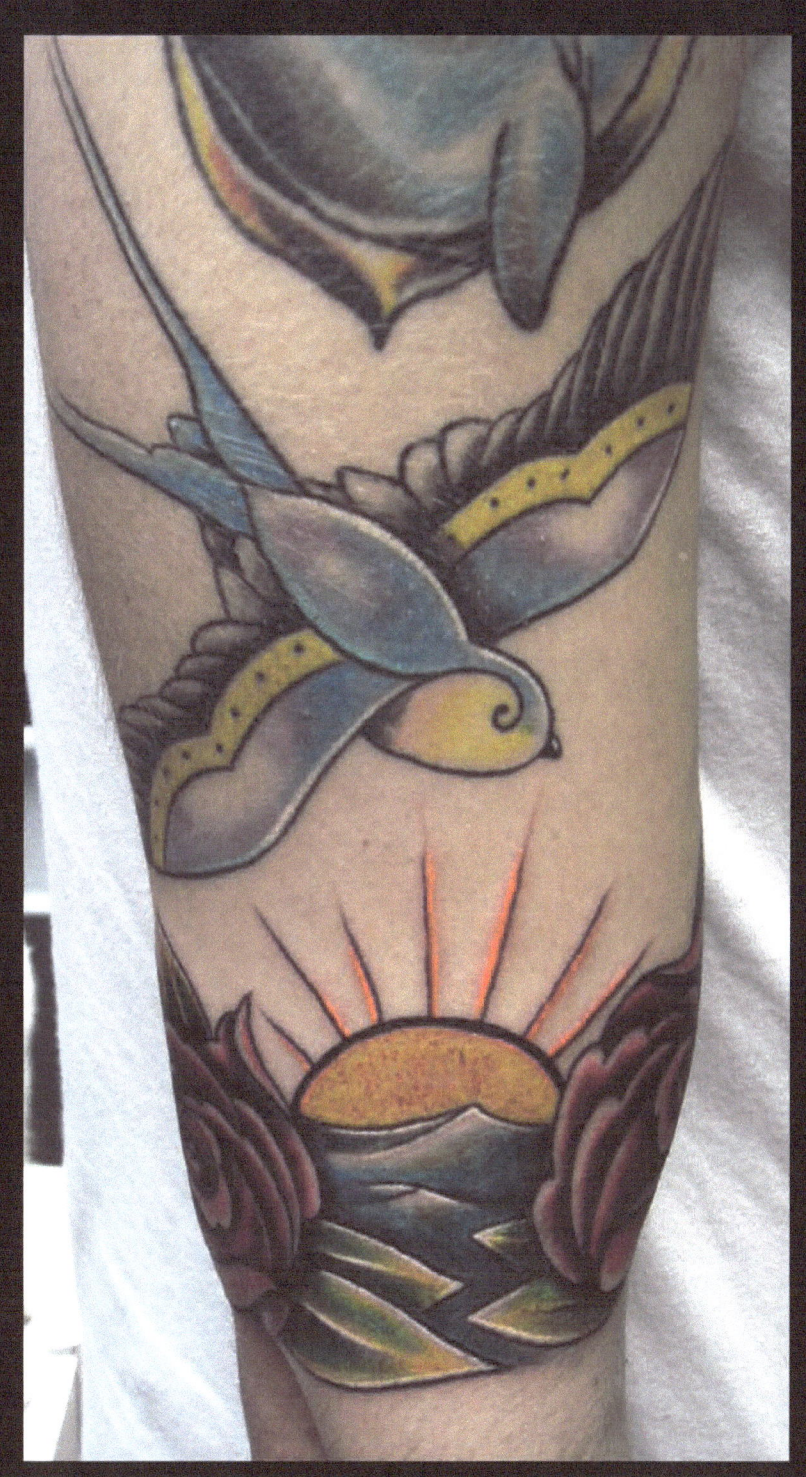

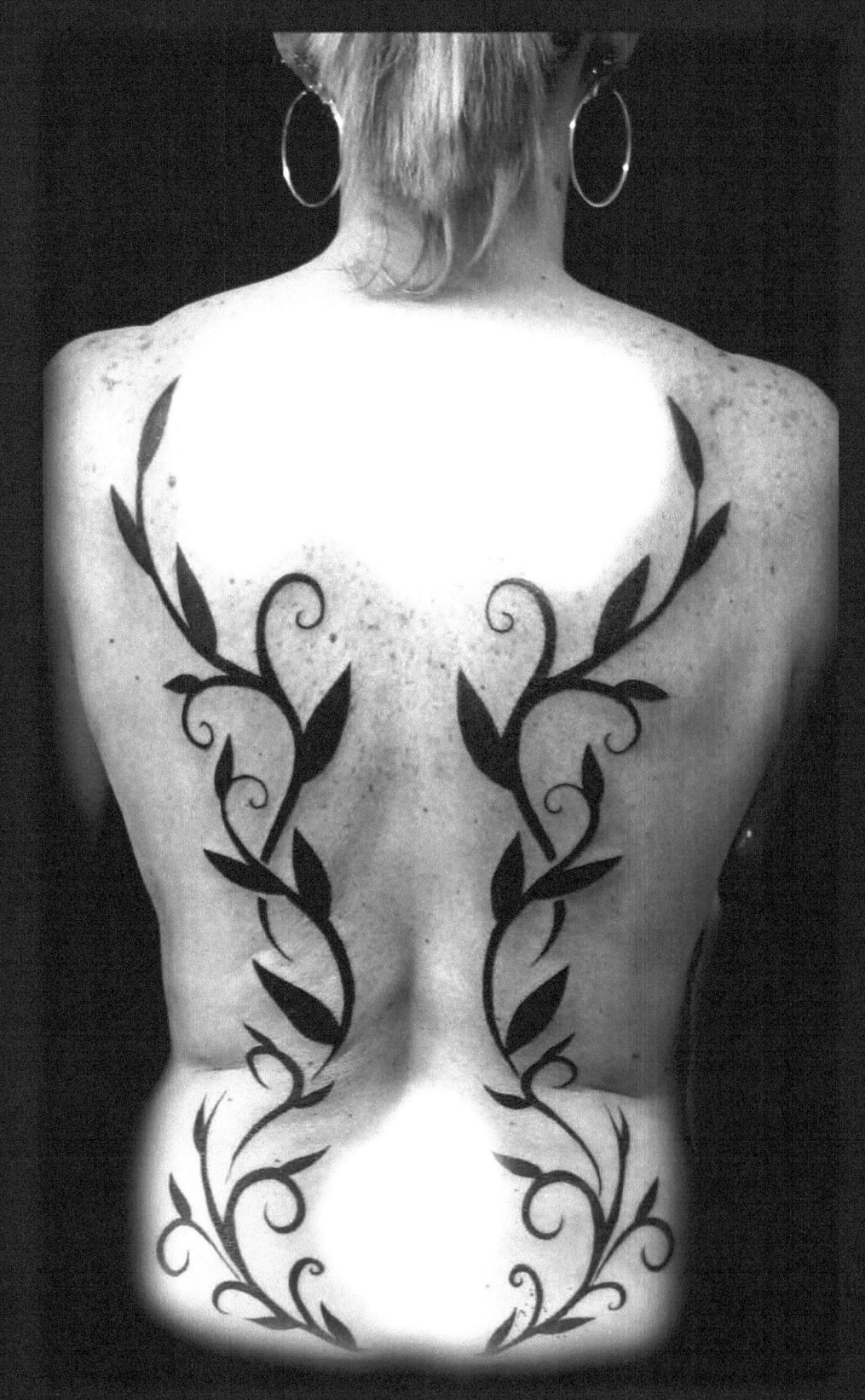

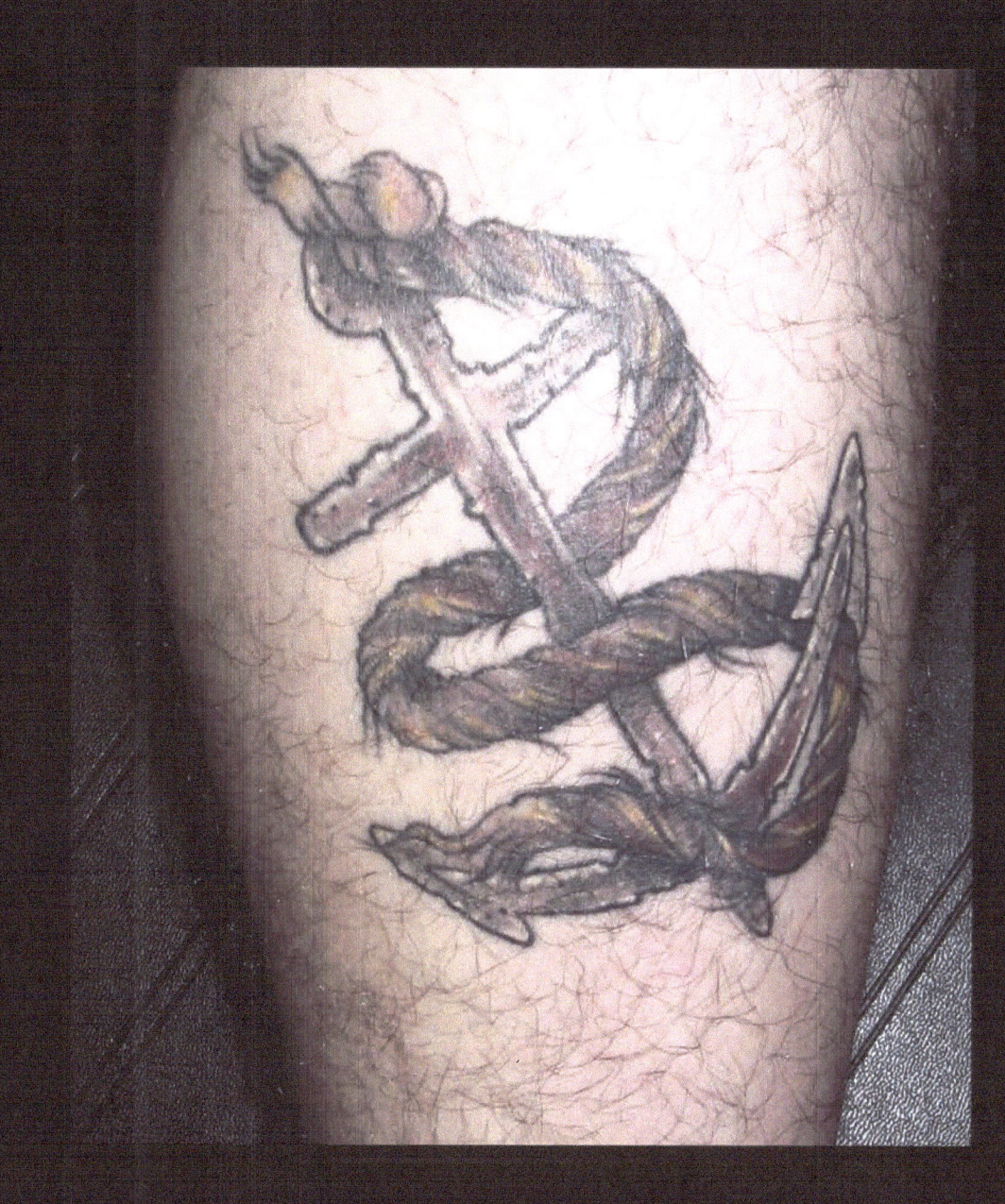

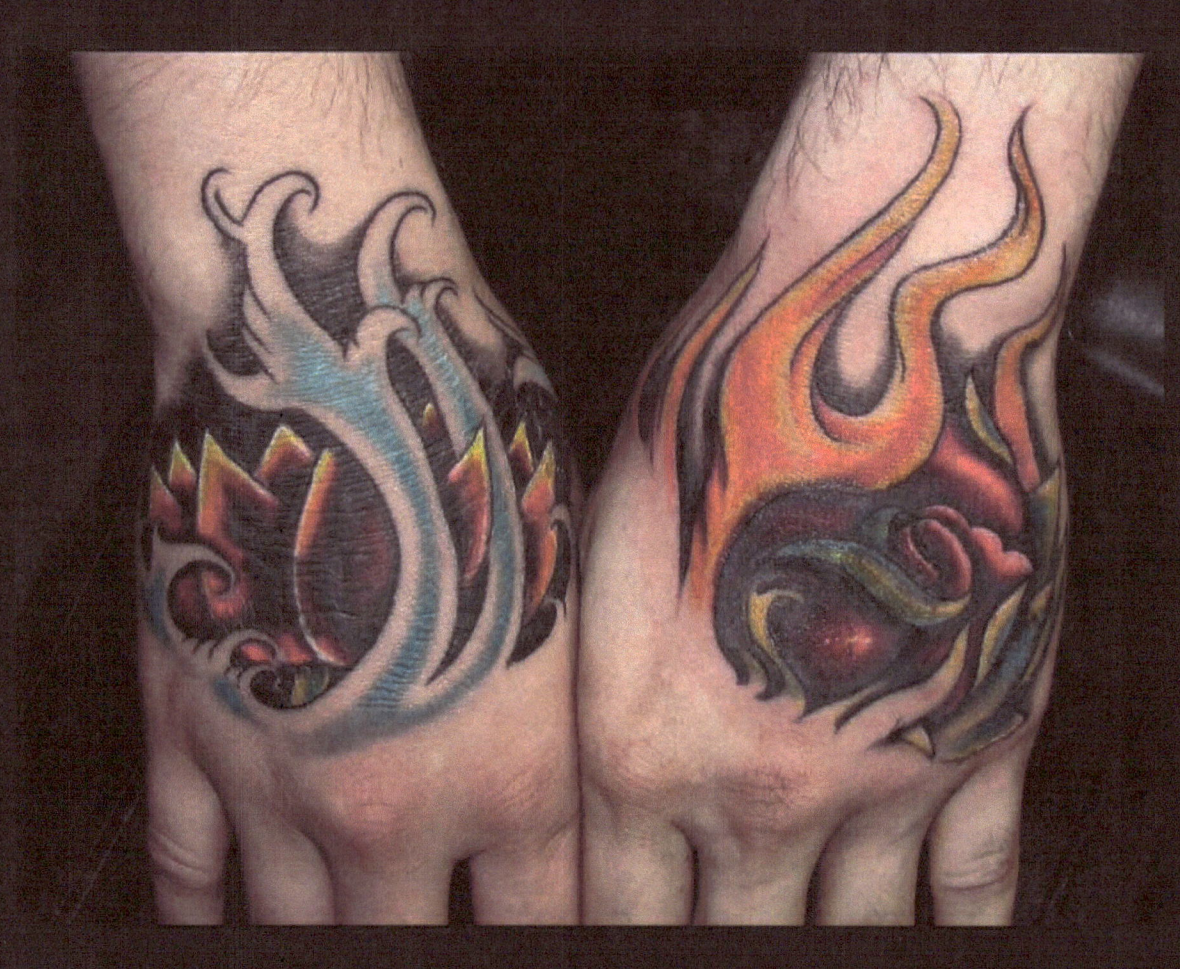

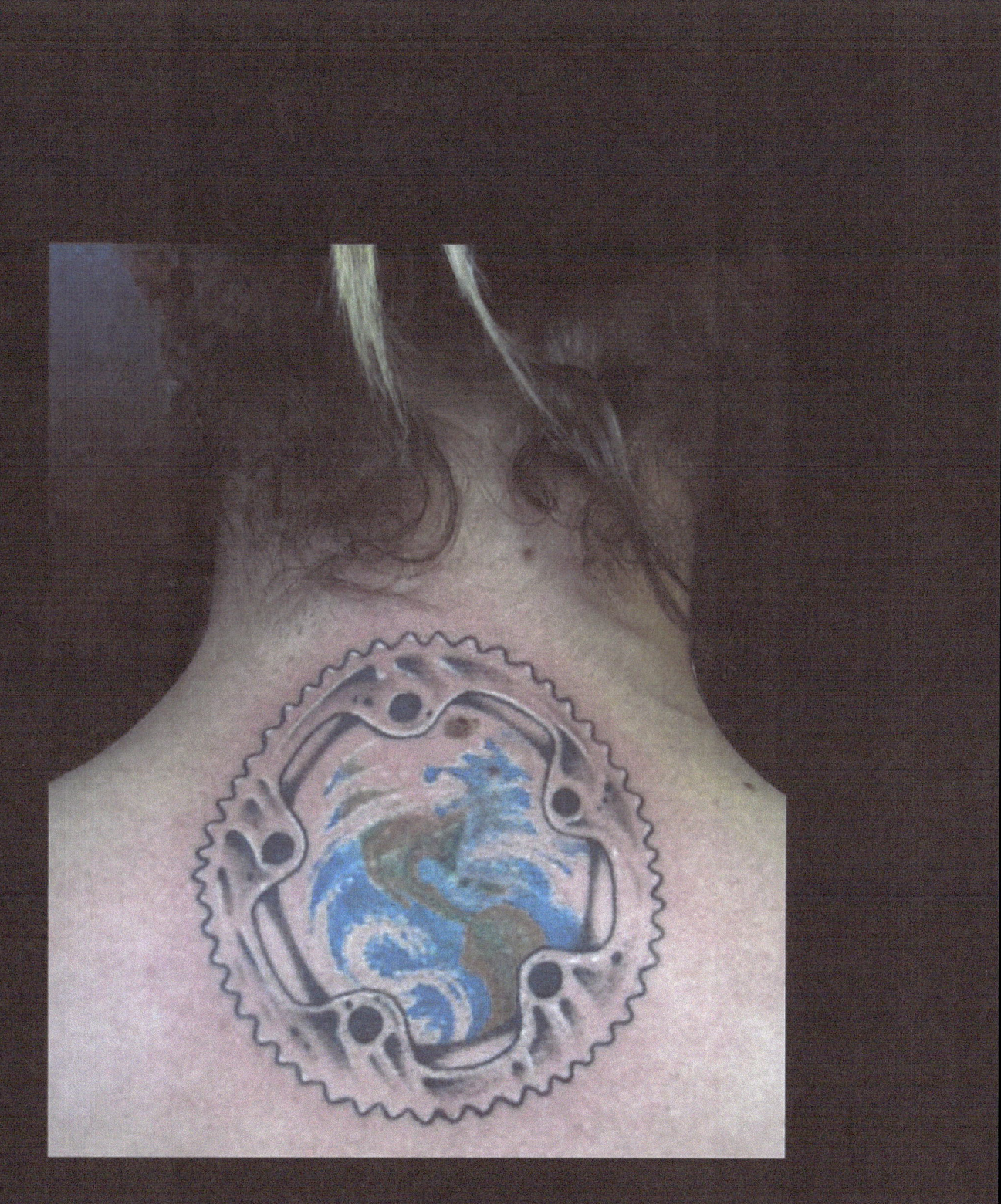

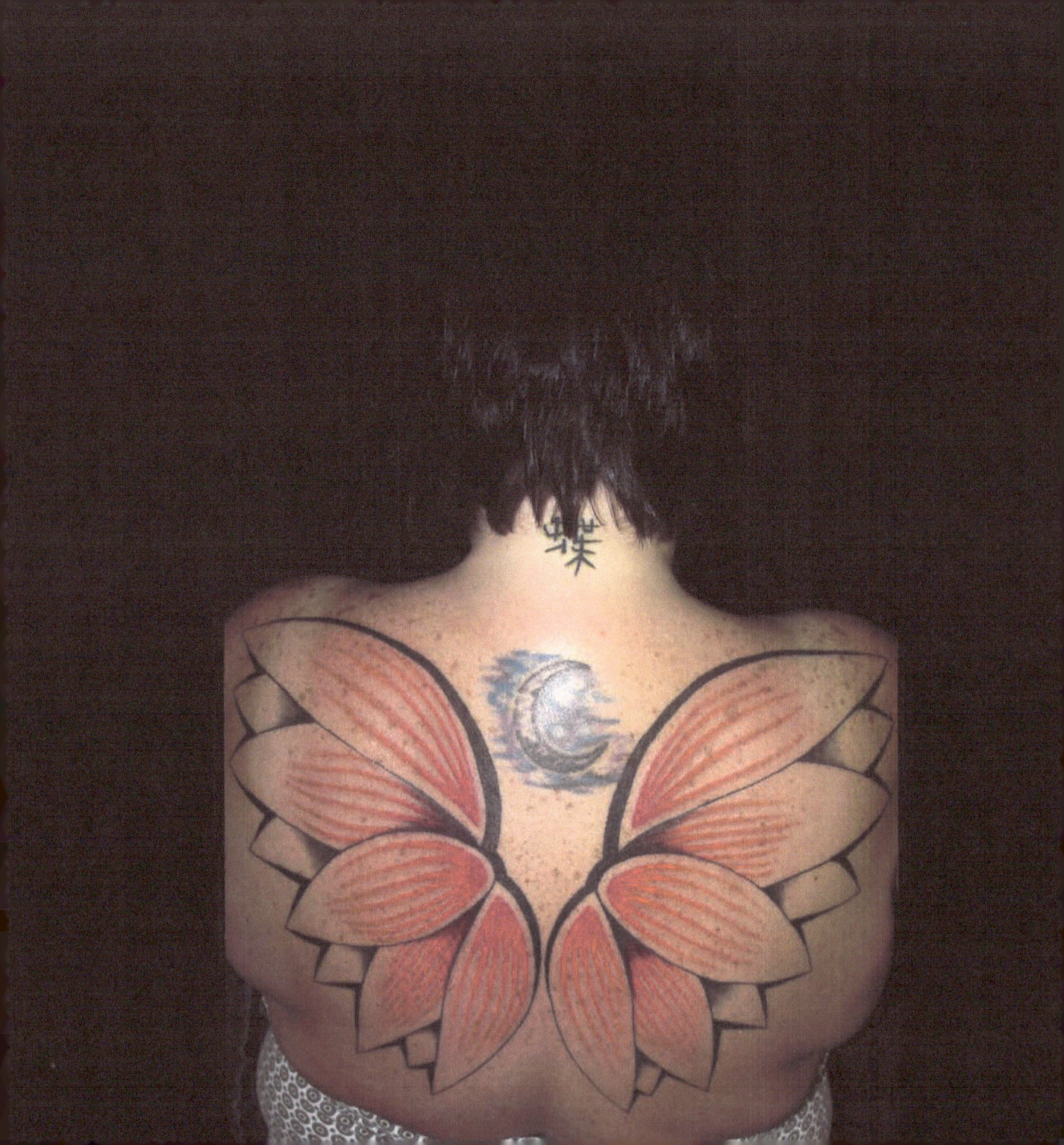

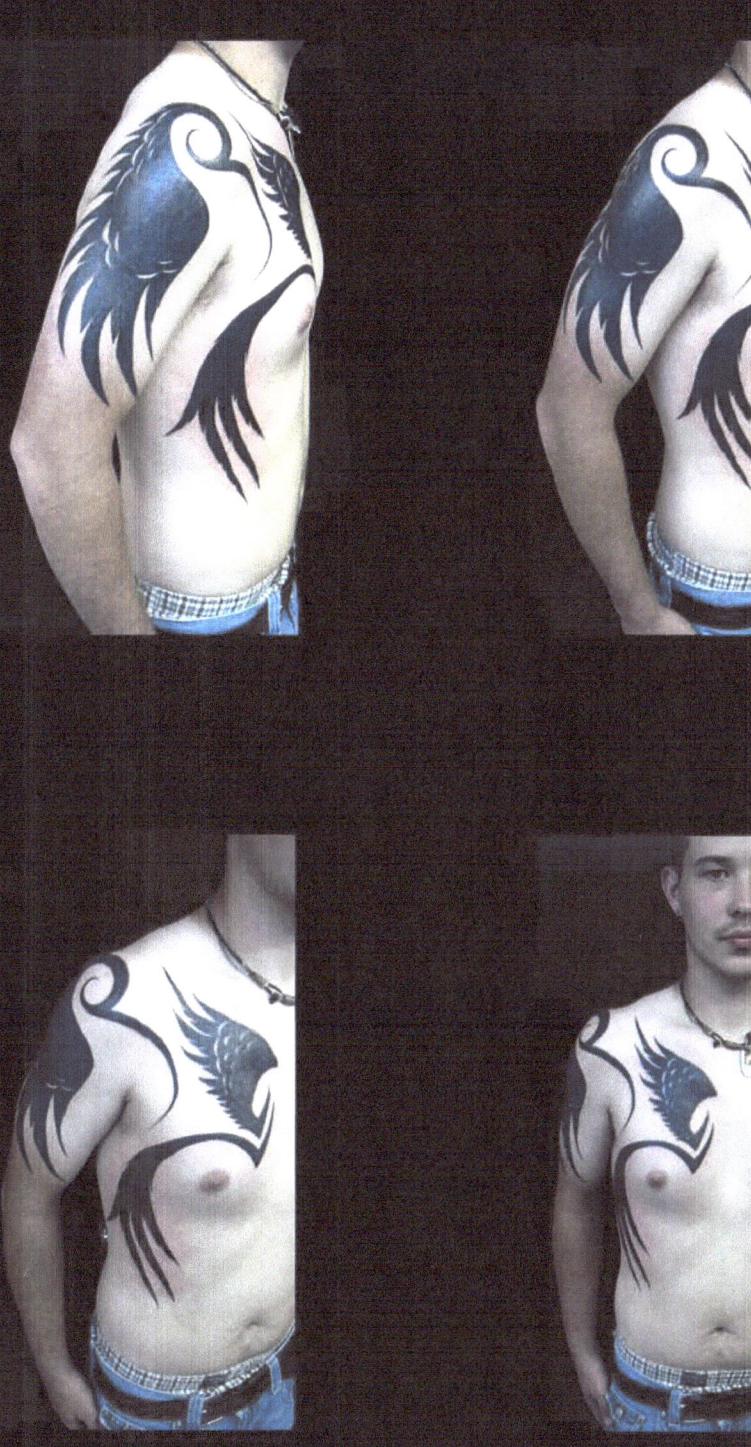

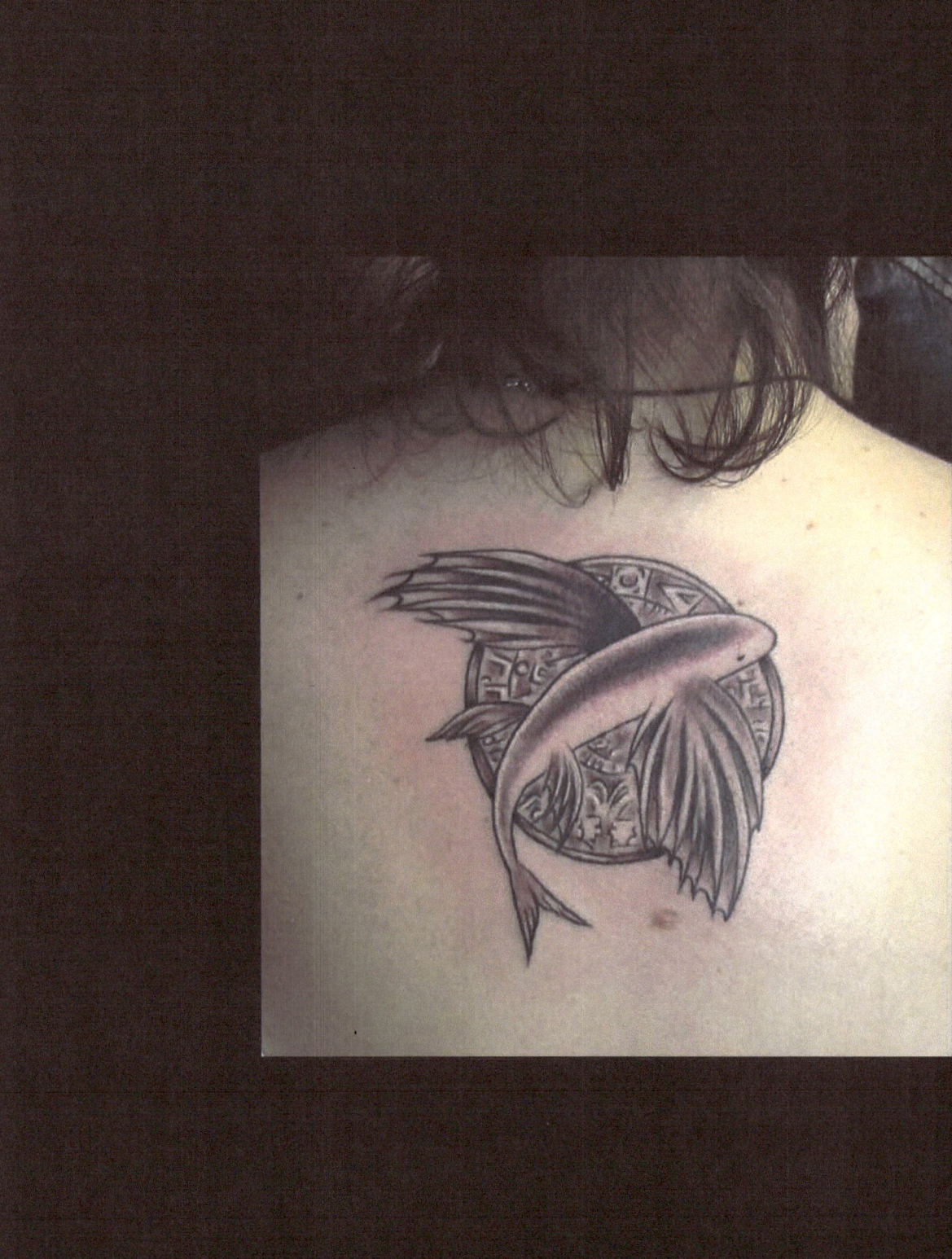

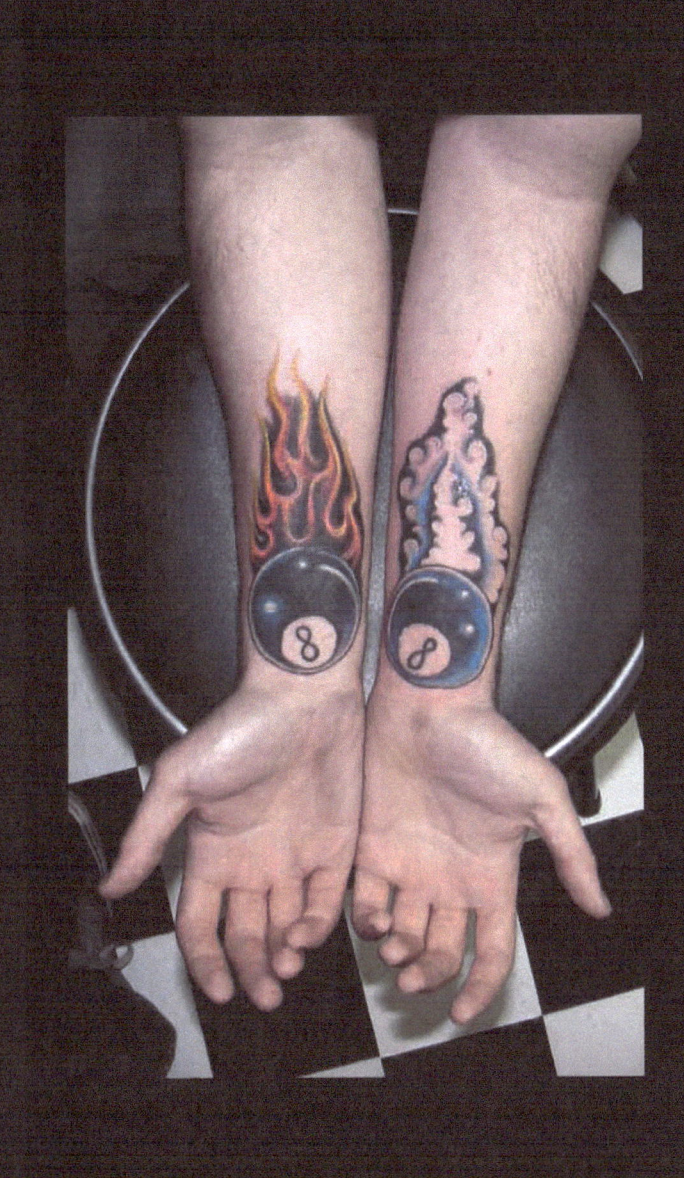

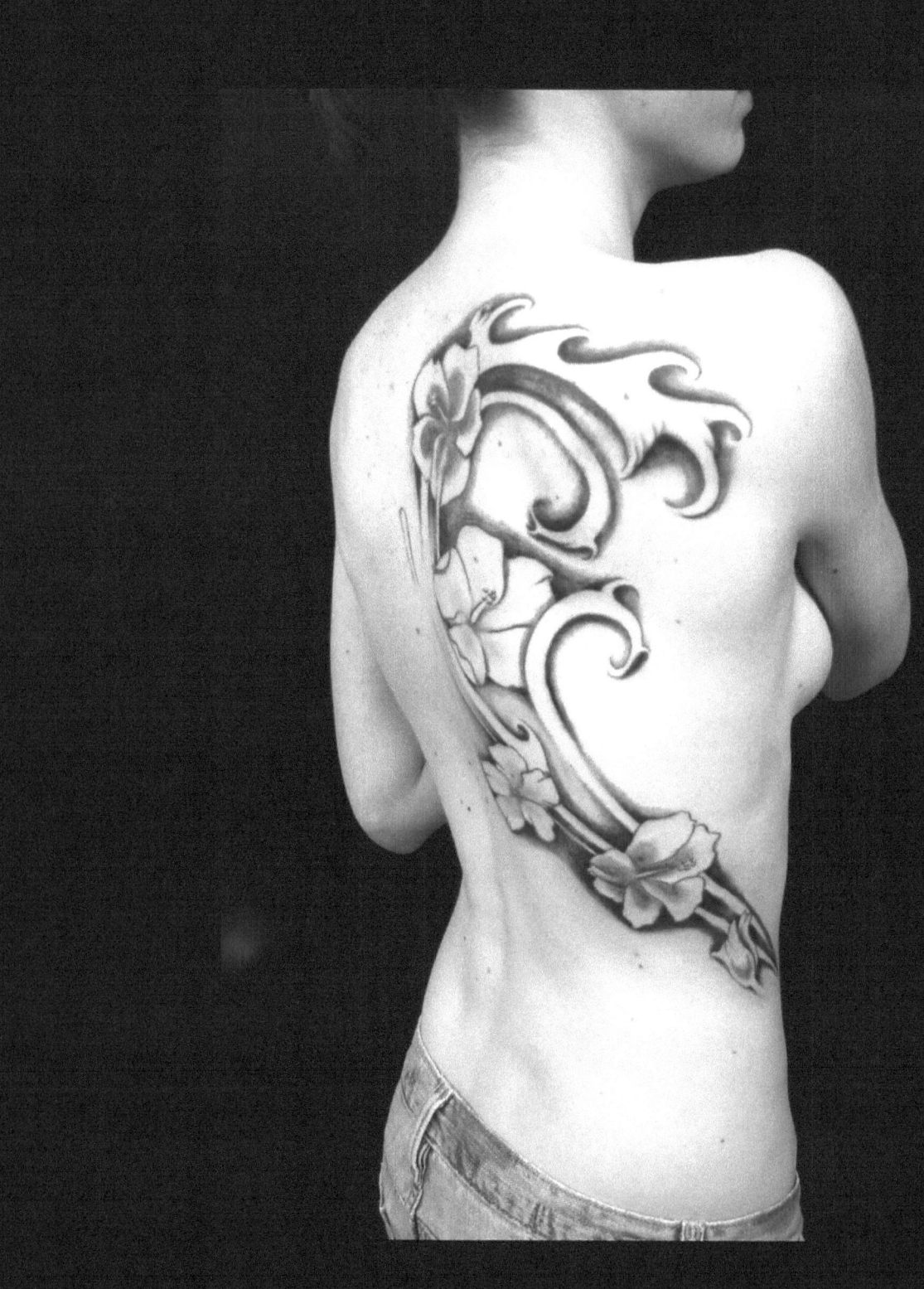

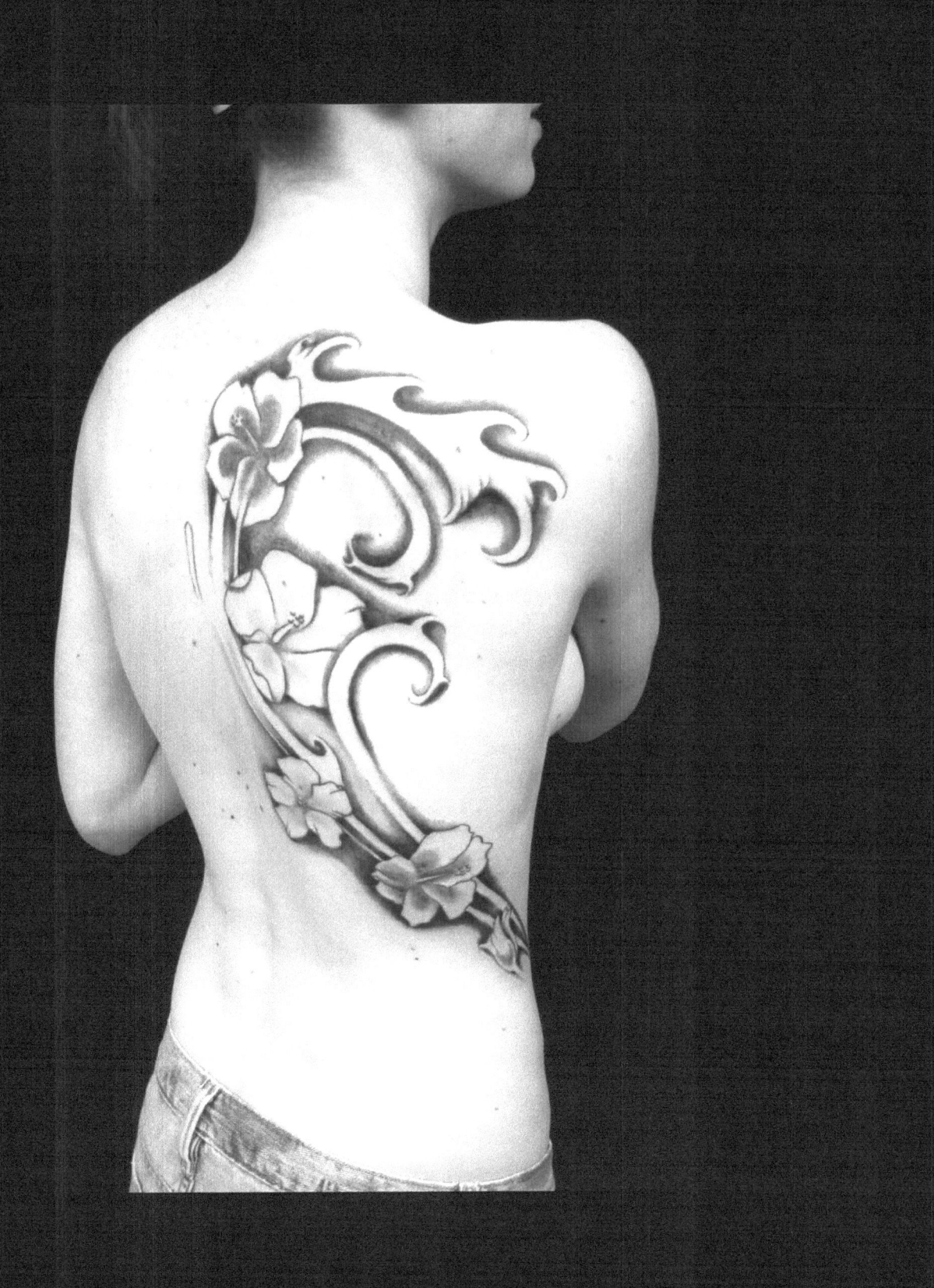

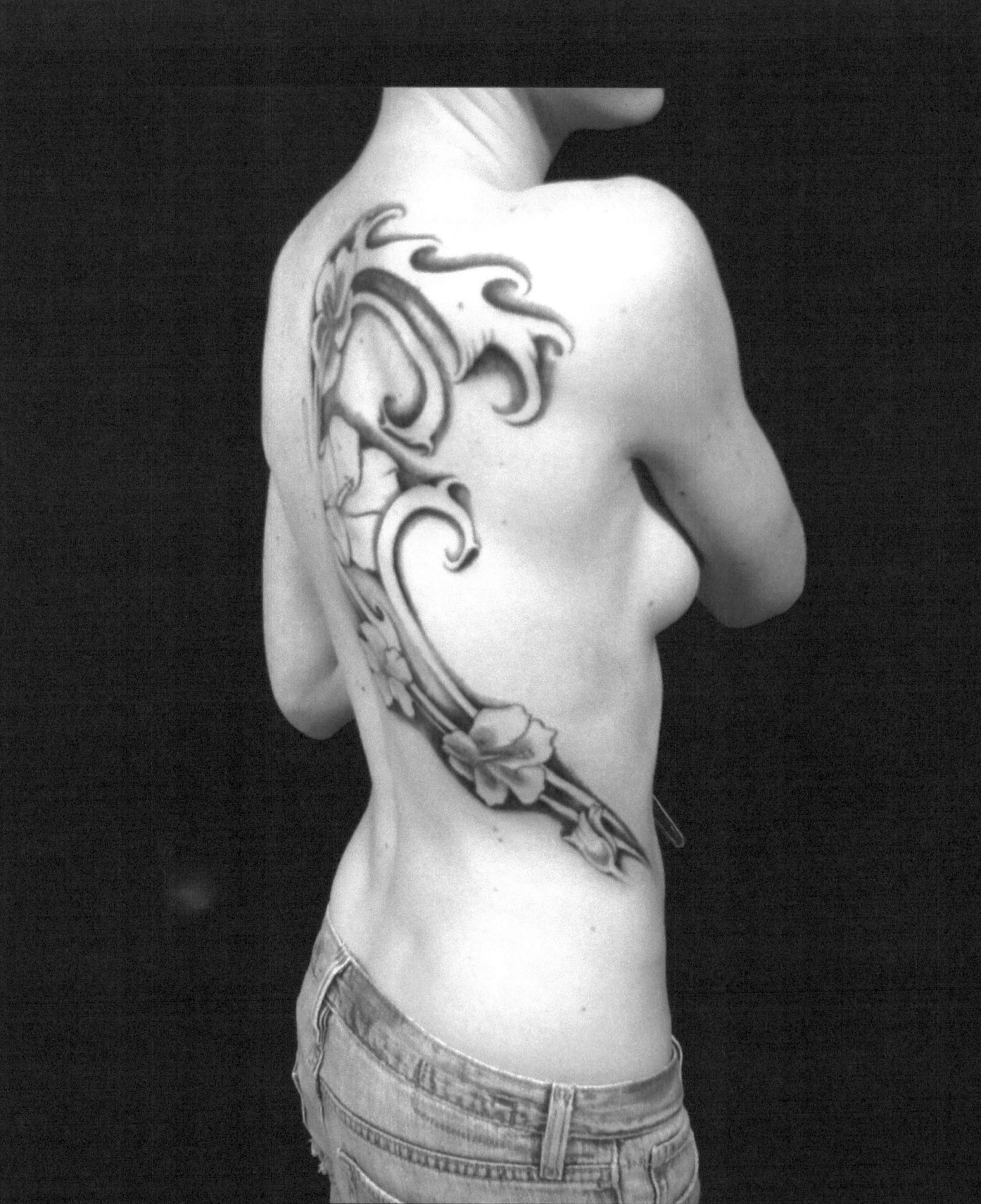

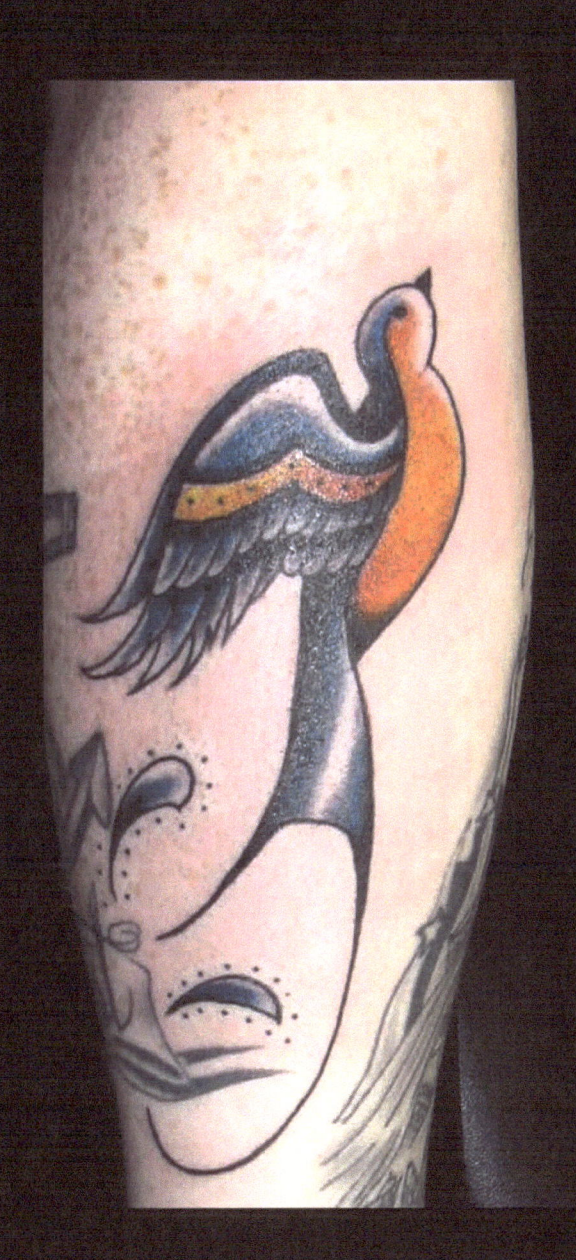

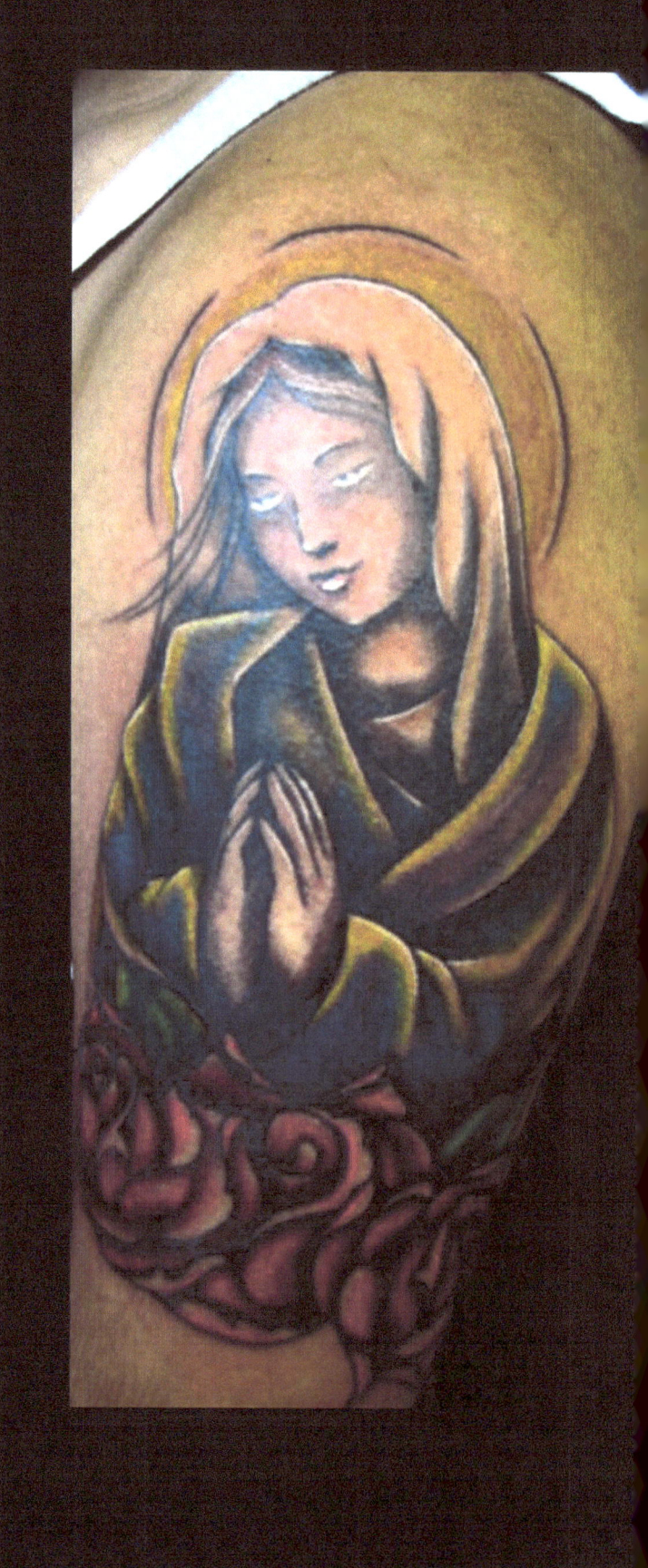

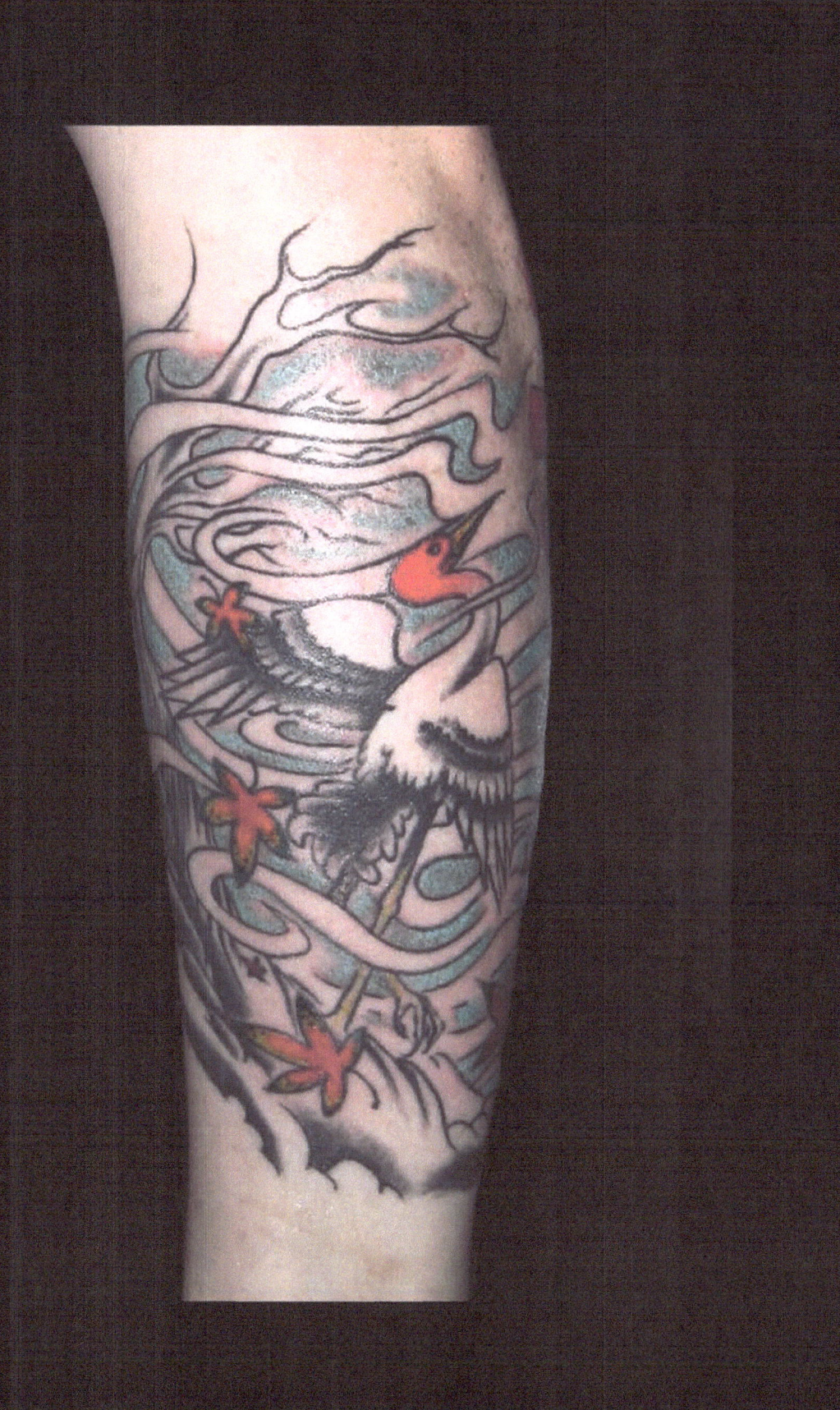

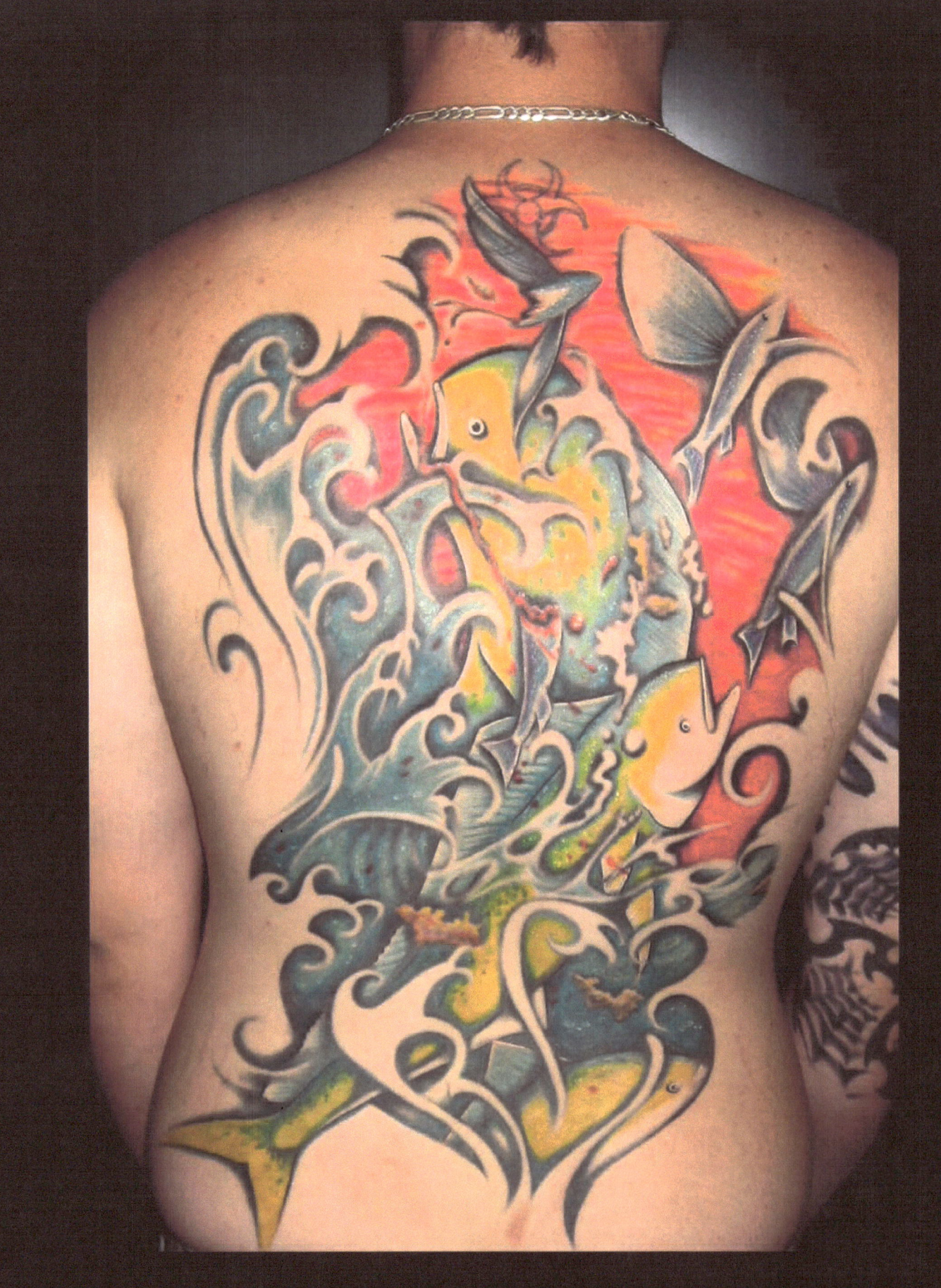

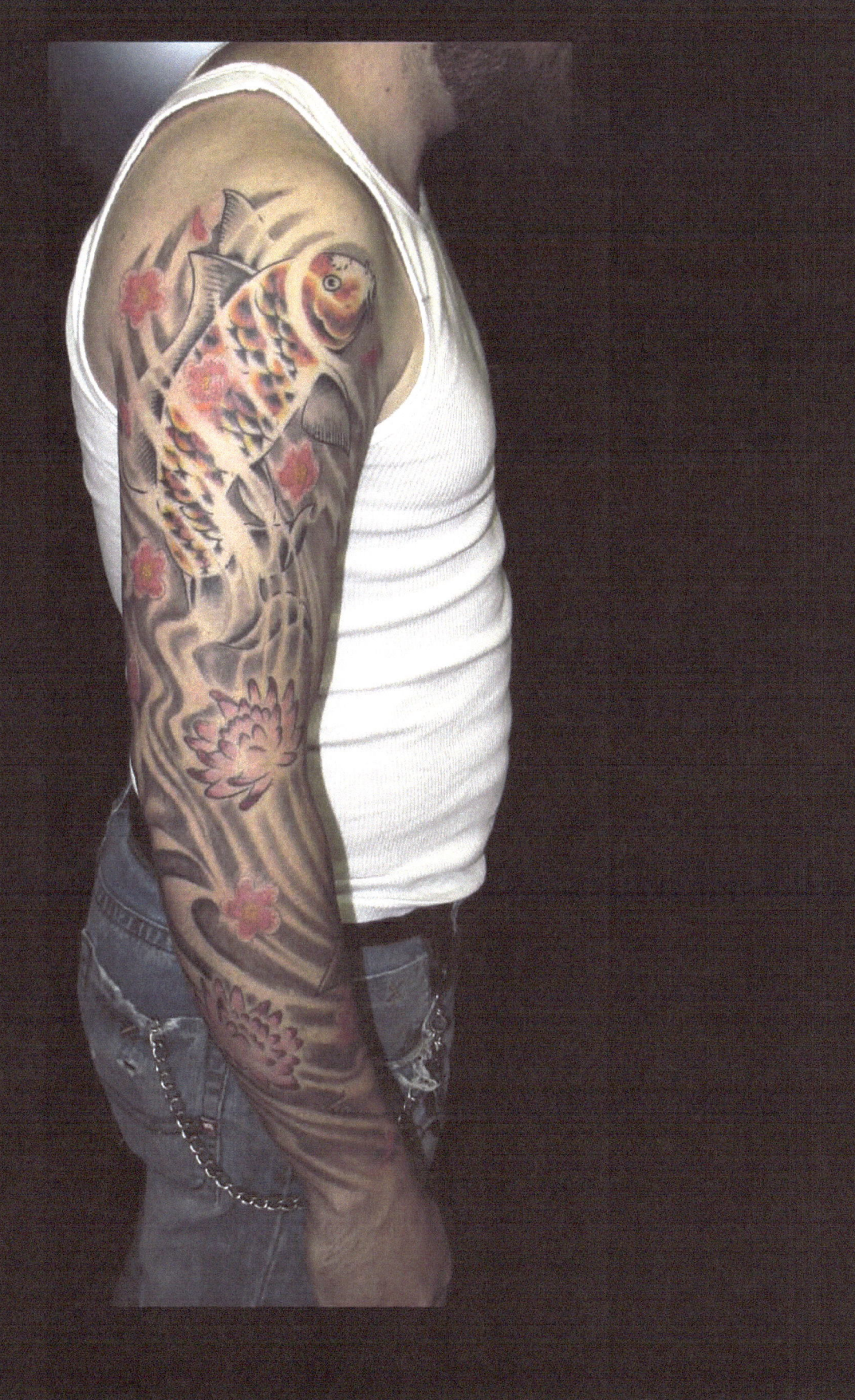

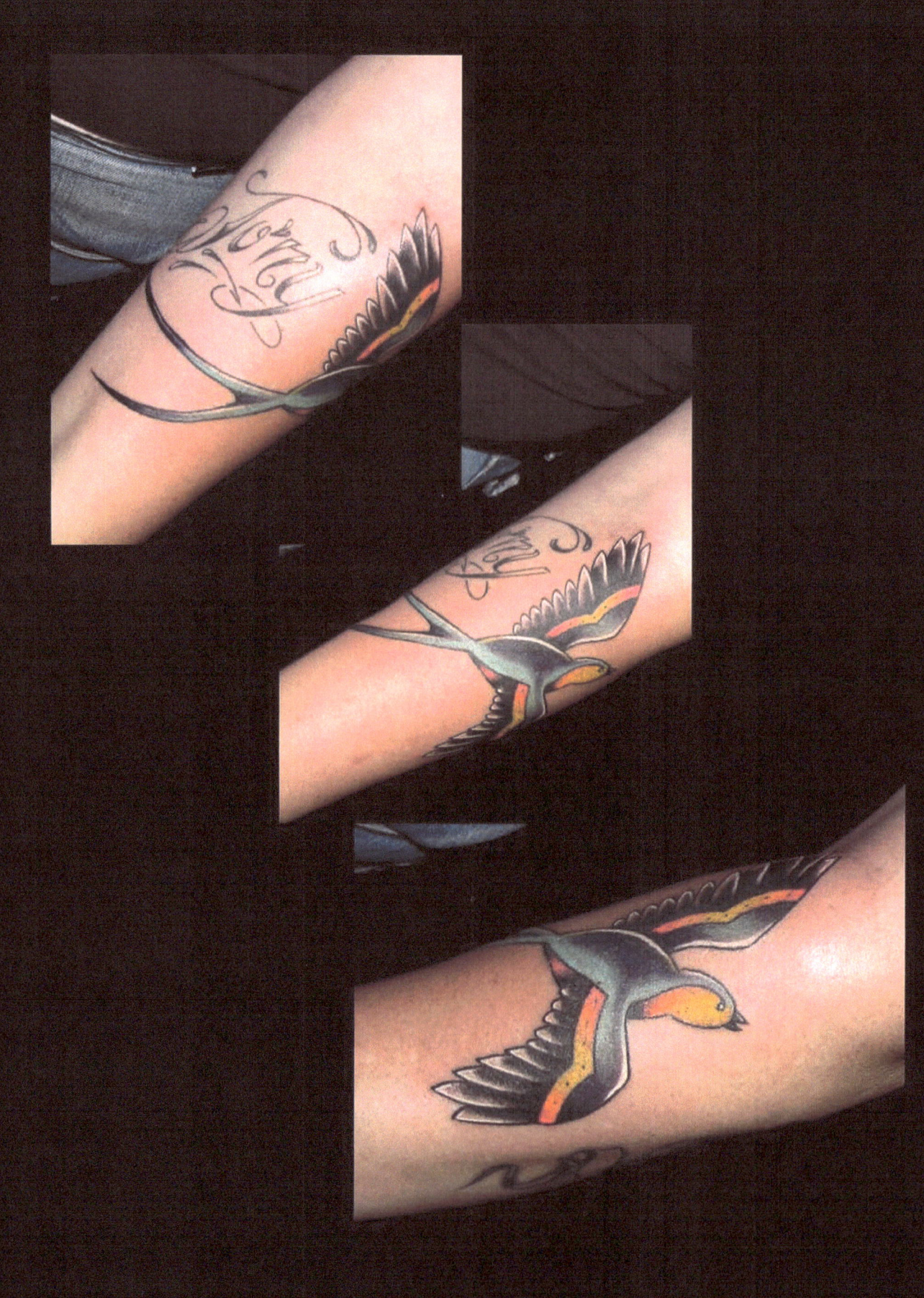

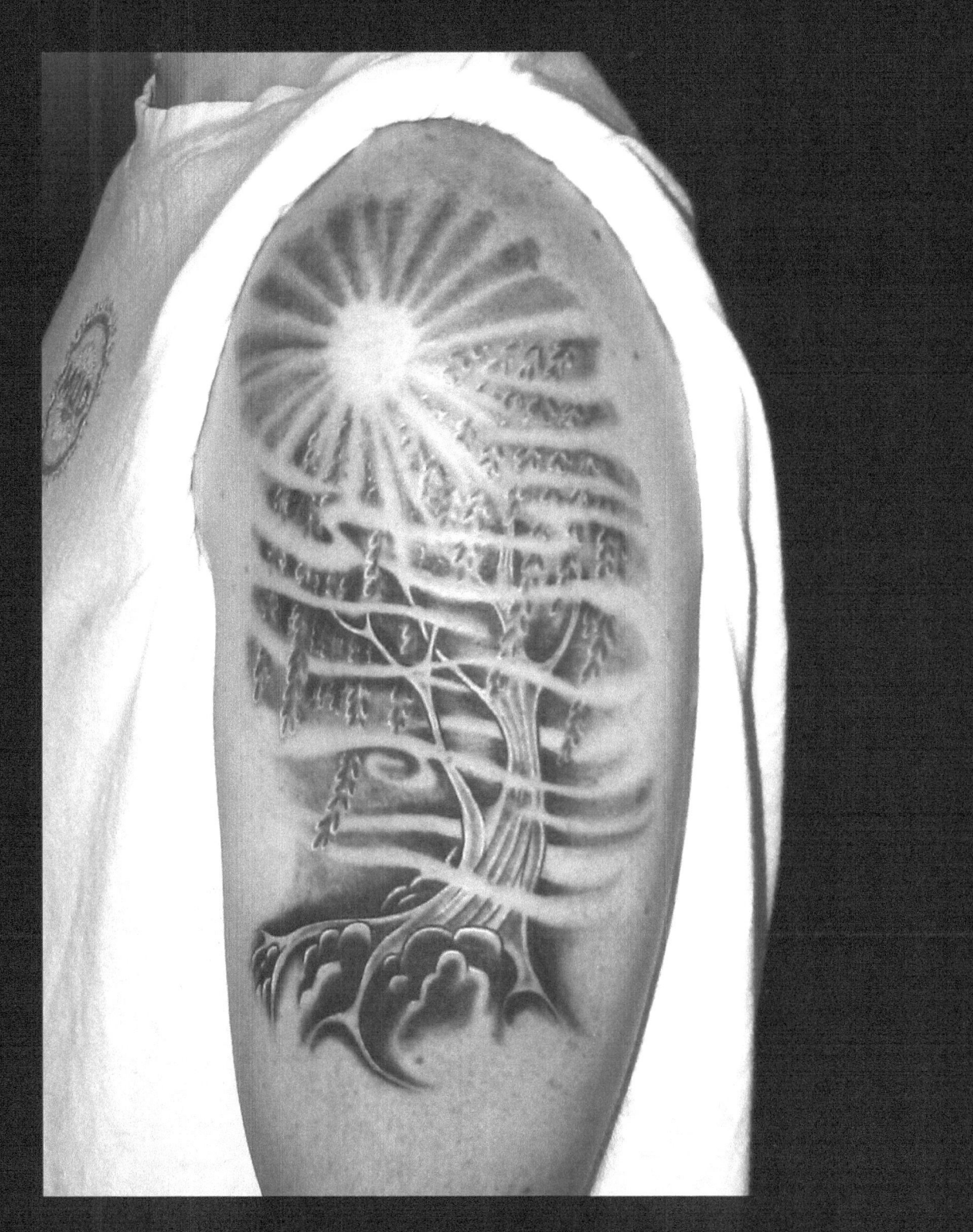

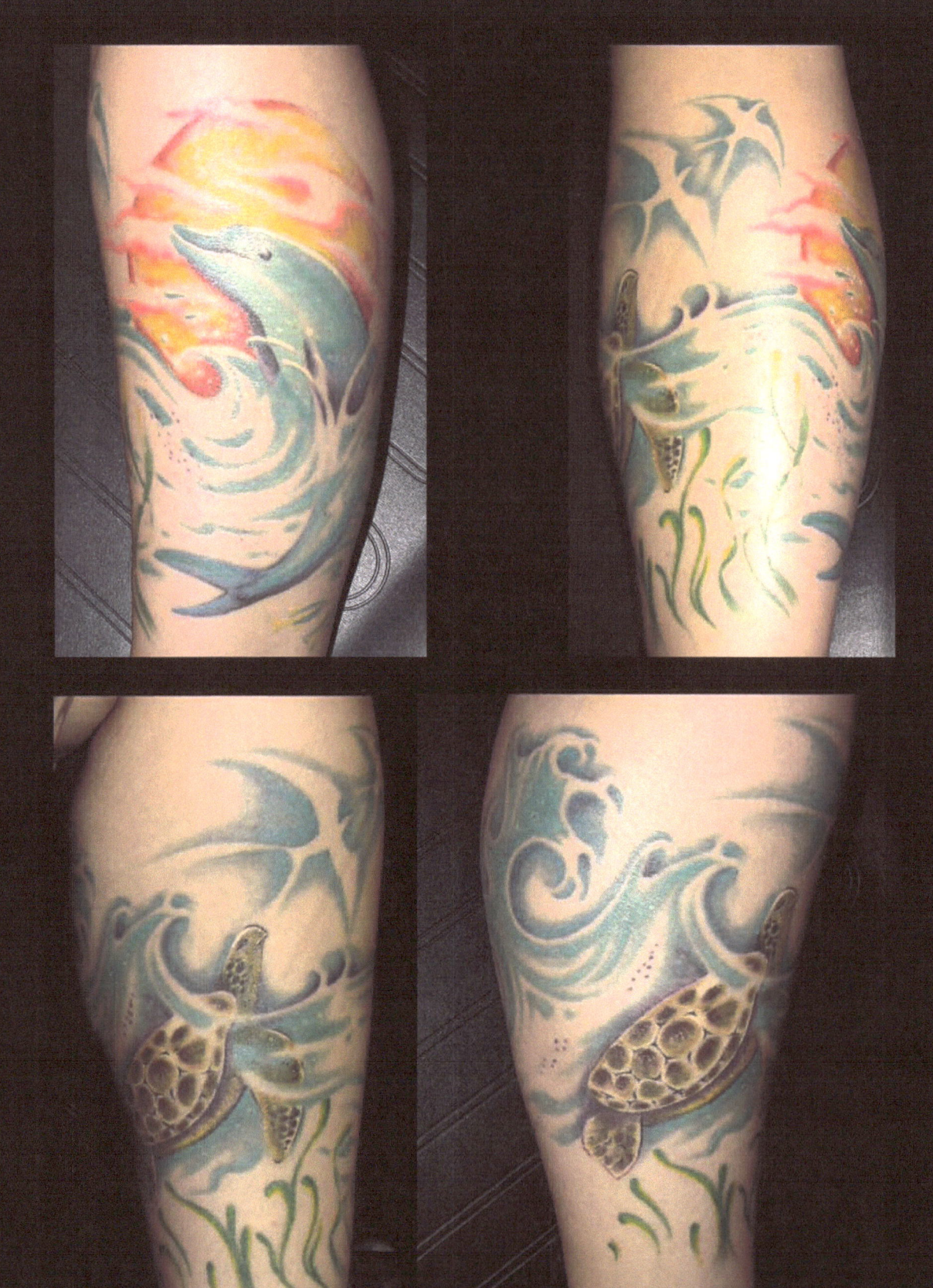

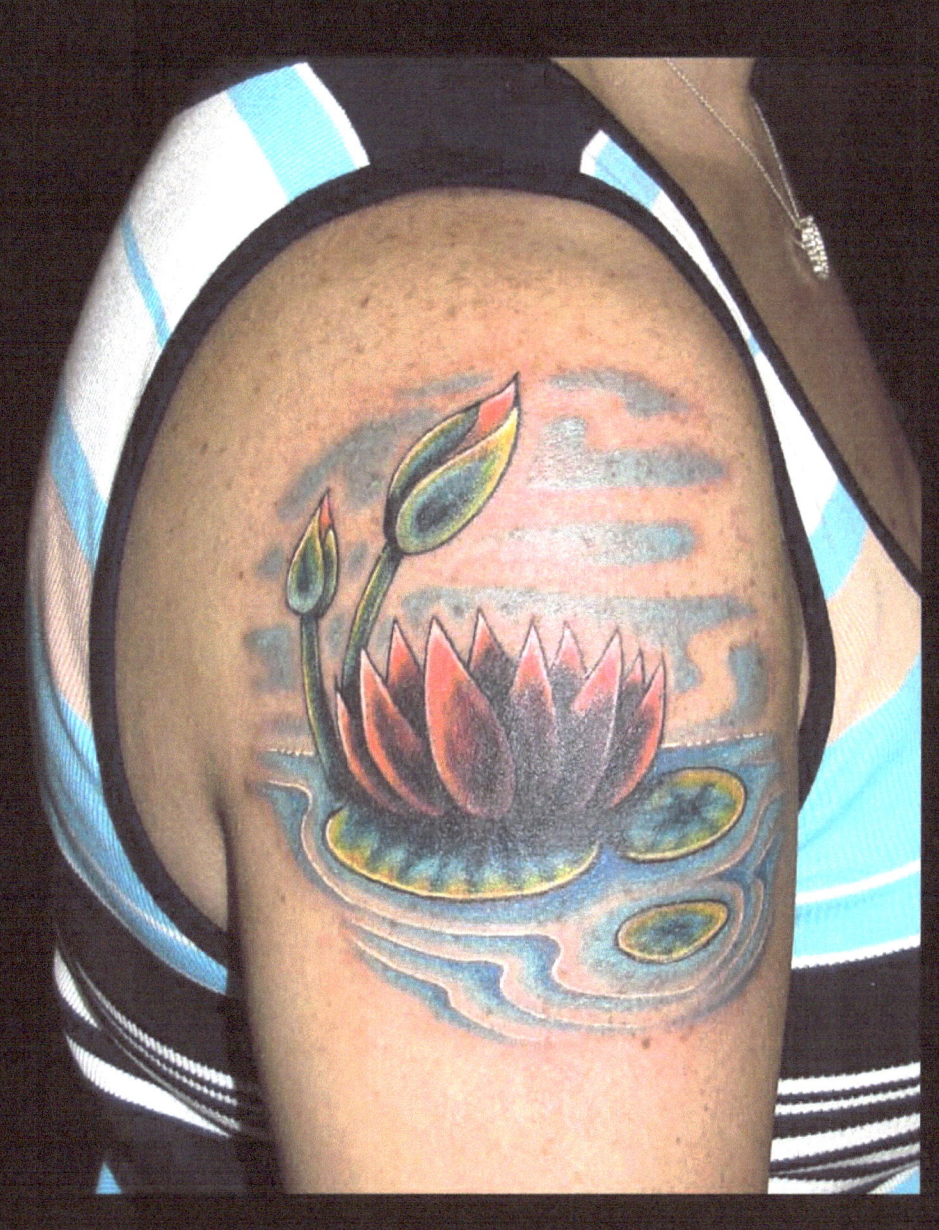

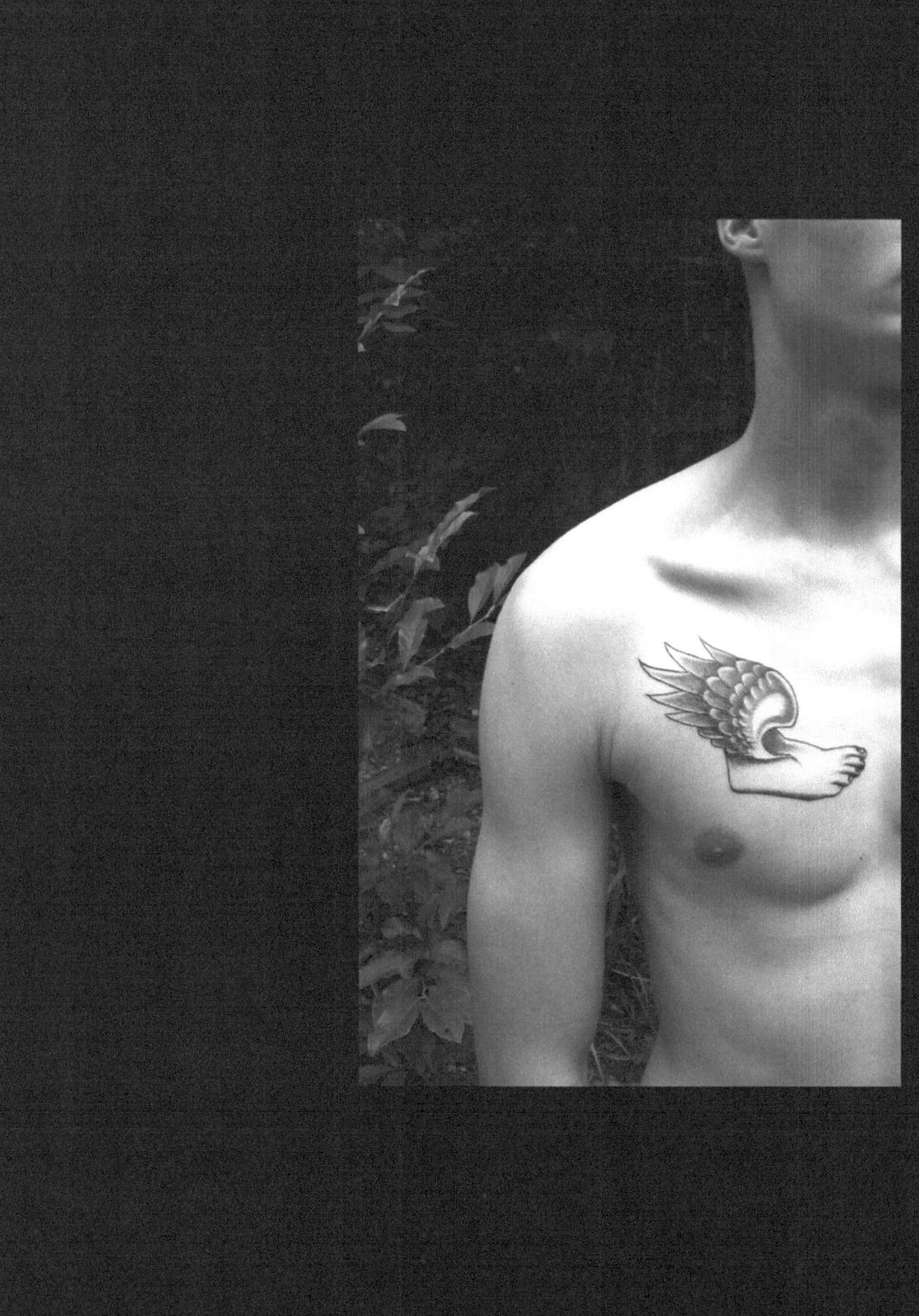

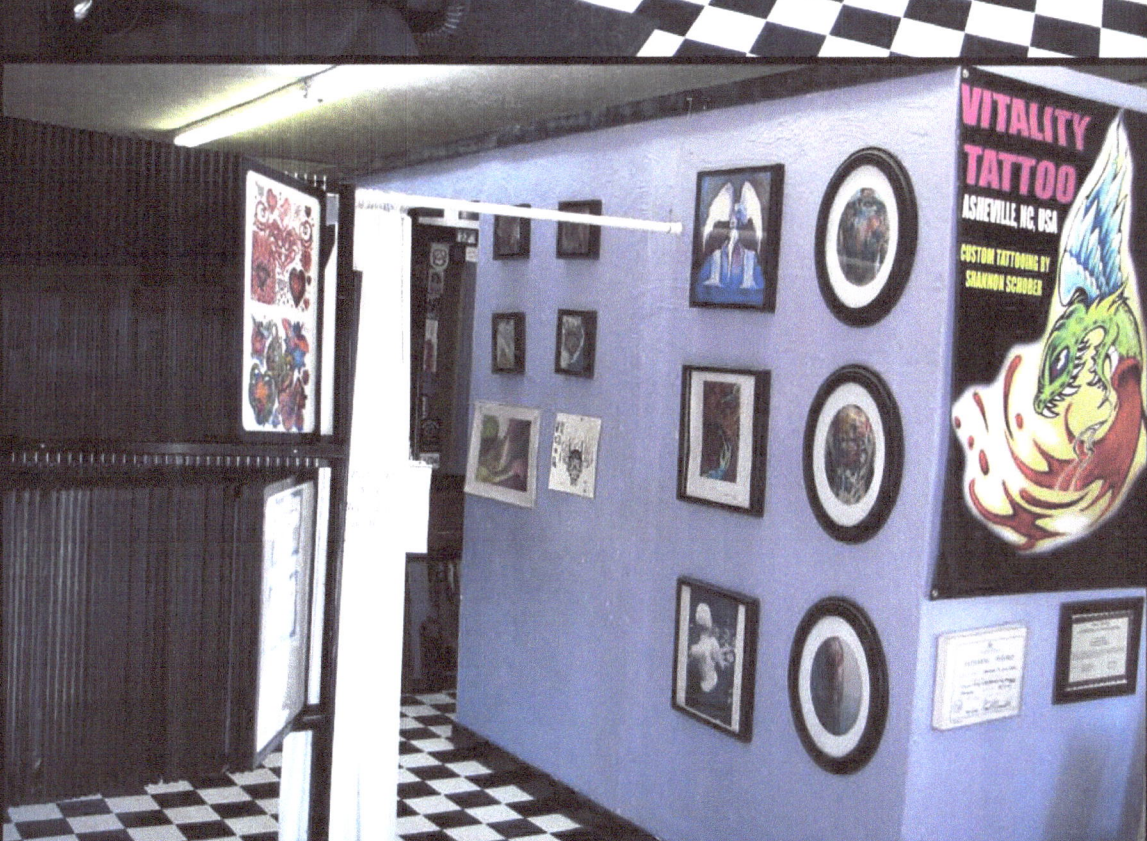

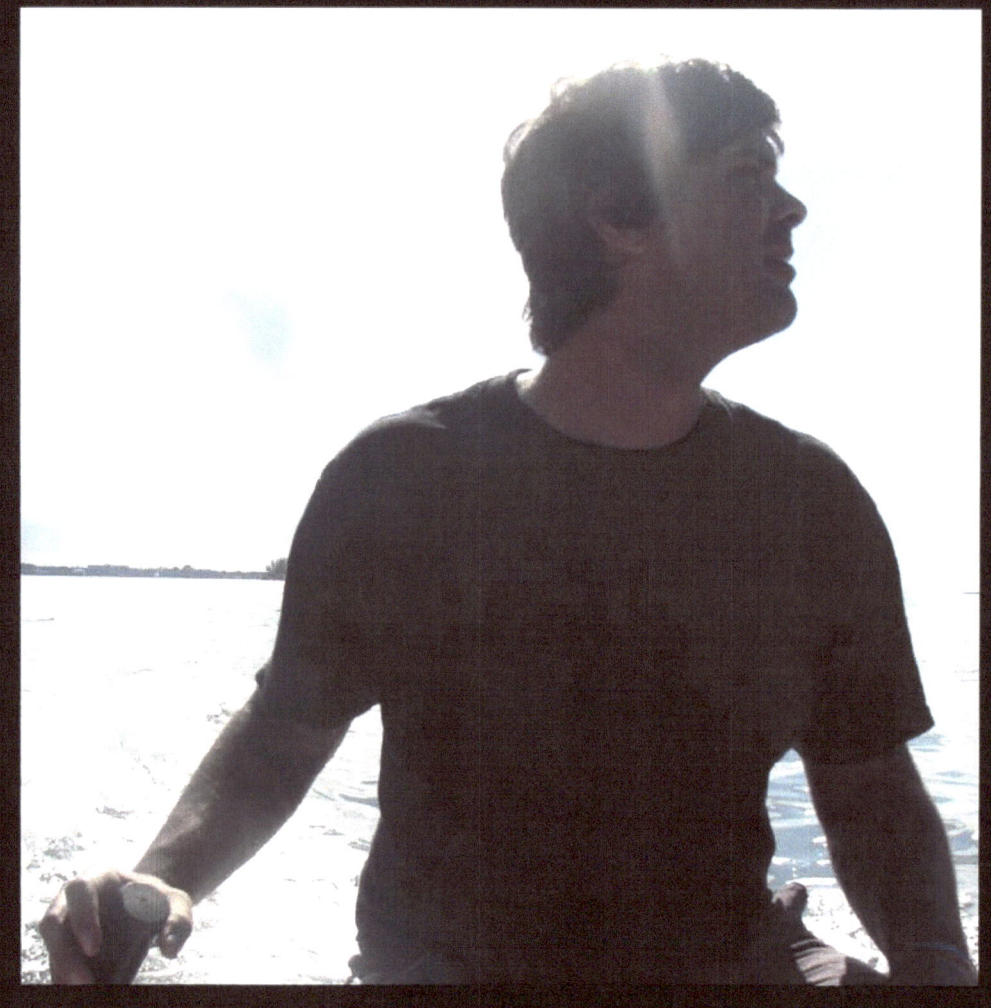

All tattoos and photos by
Shannon Schober
(c) 2009

www.ingramcontent.com/pod-product-compliance
Lightning Source LLC
Chambersburg PA
CBHW050731180526
45159CB00003B/1190